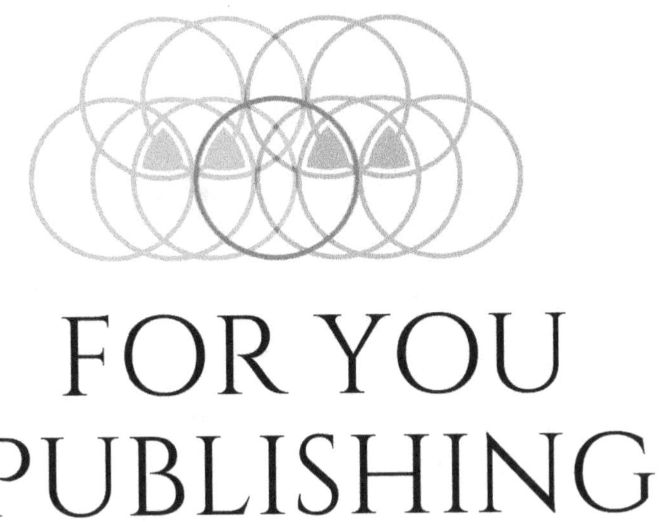

# FOR YOU
# PUBLISHING

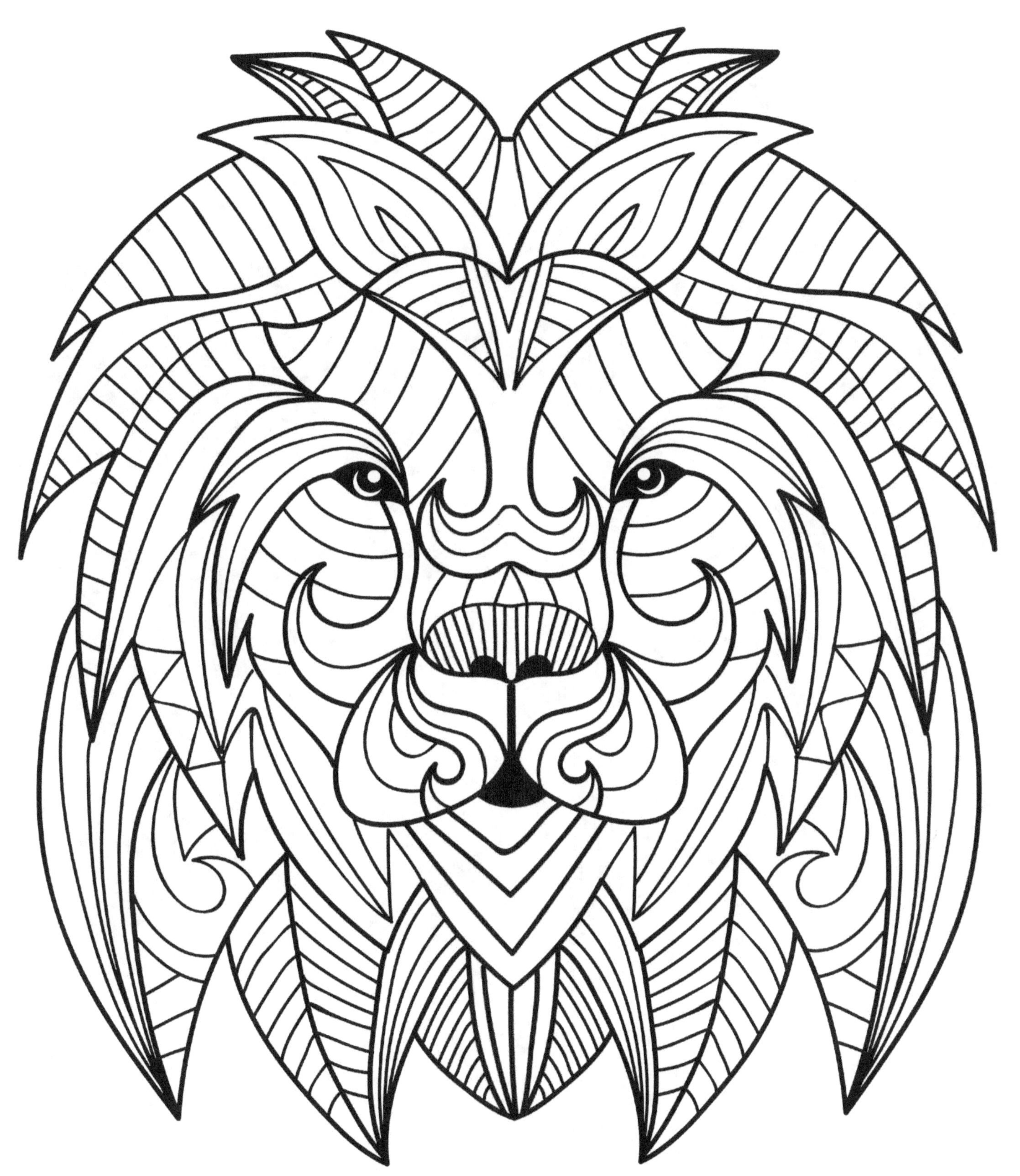

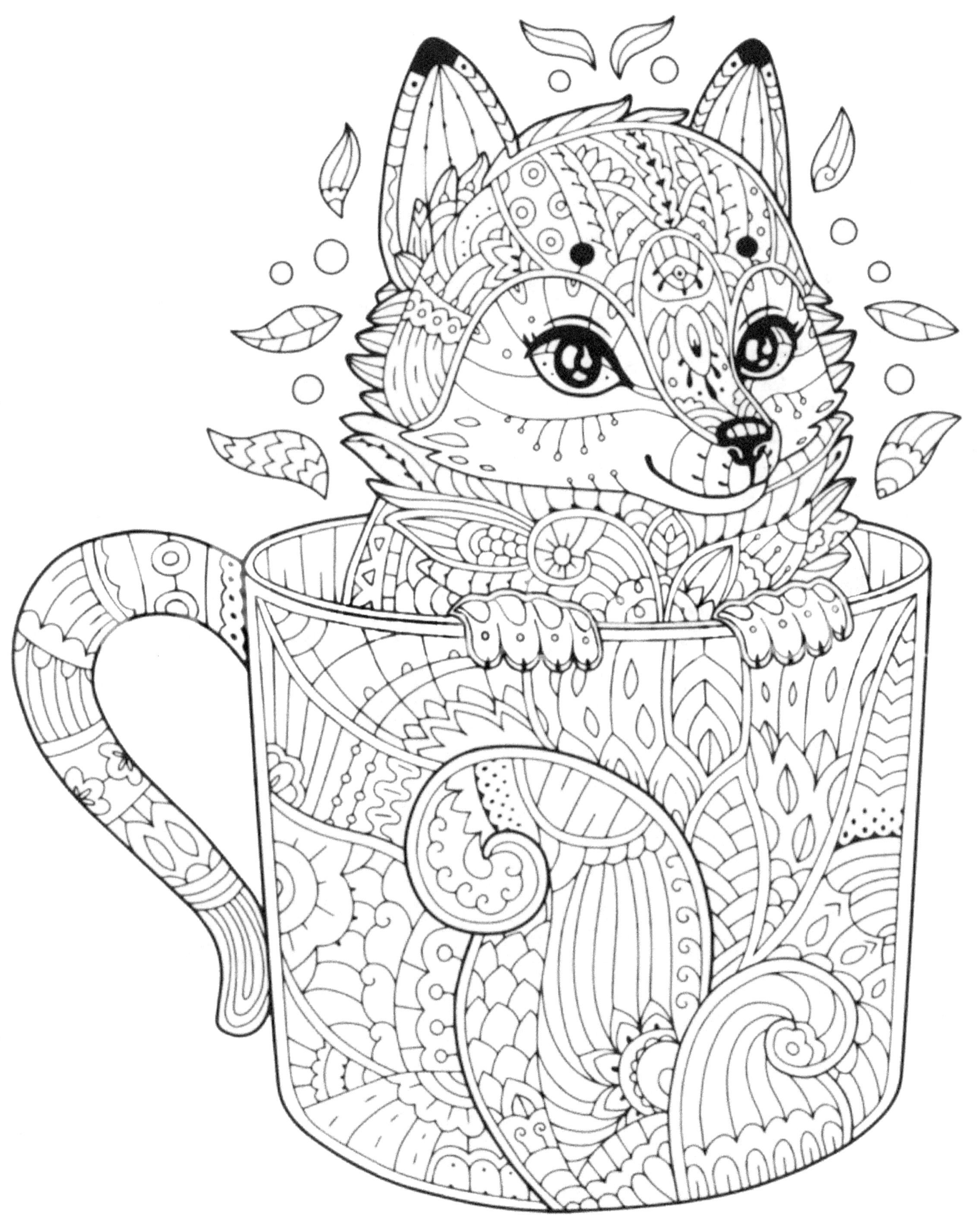

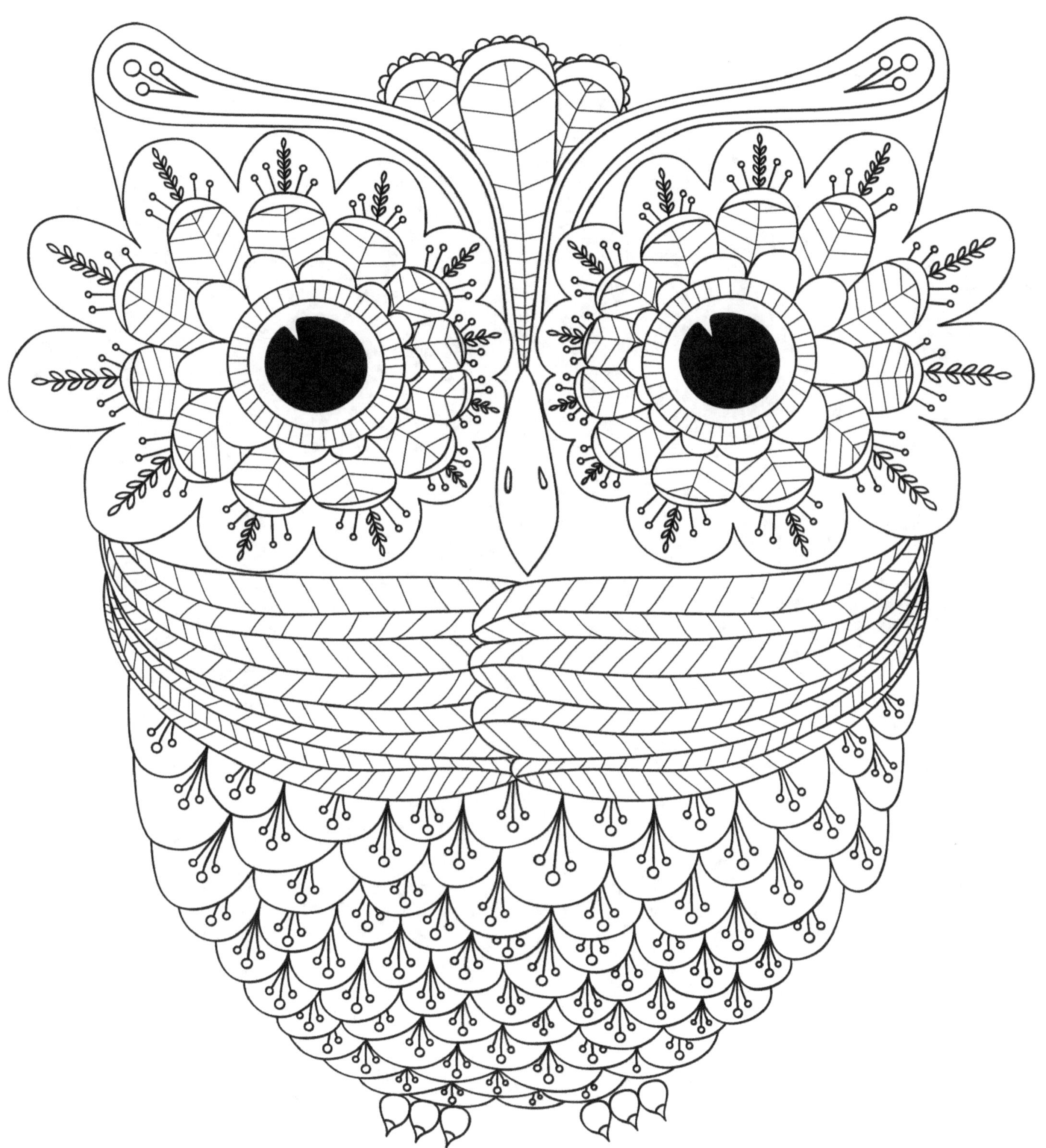

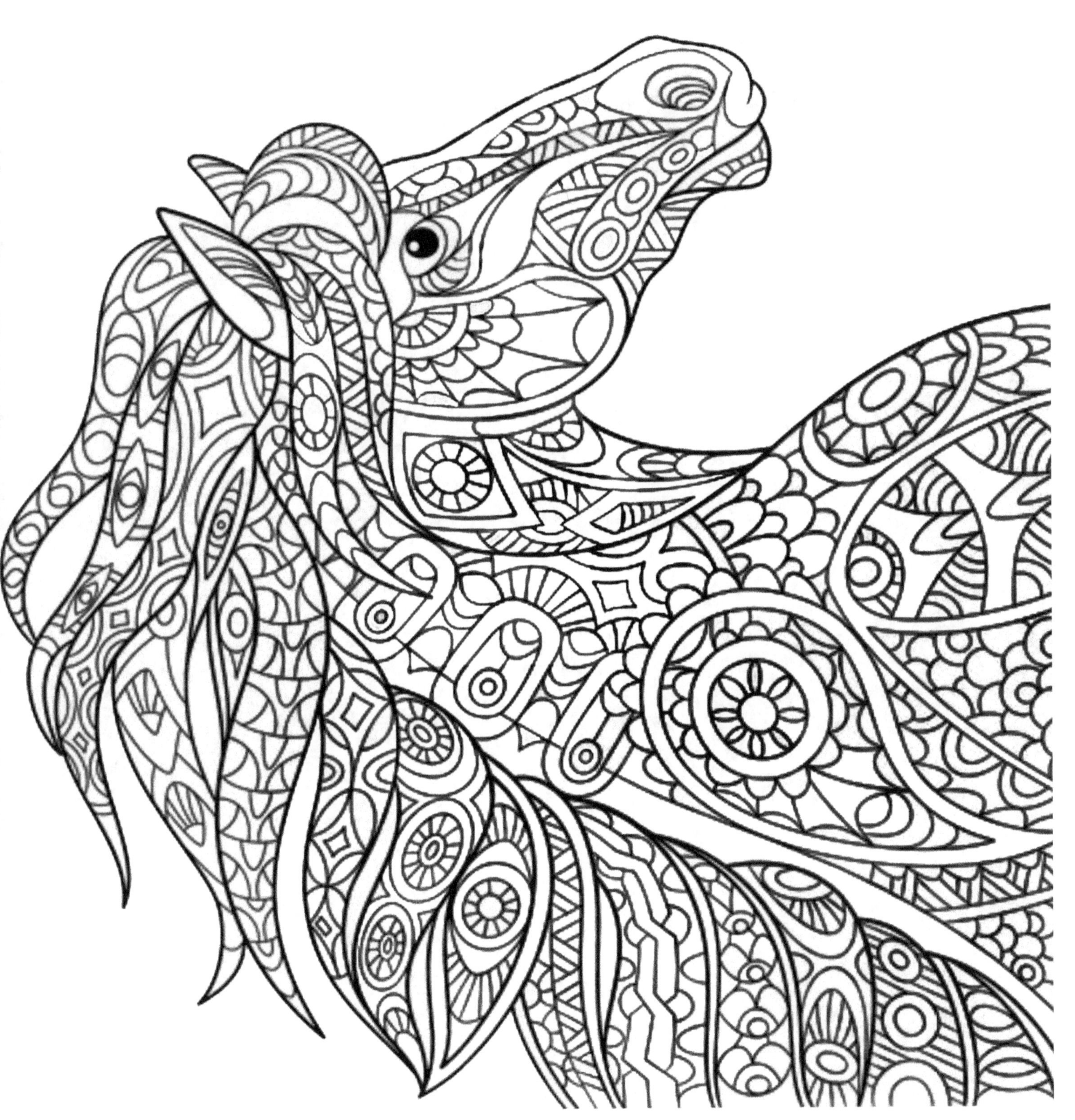

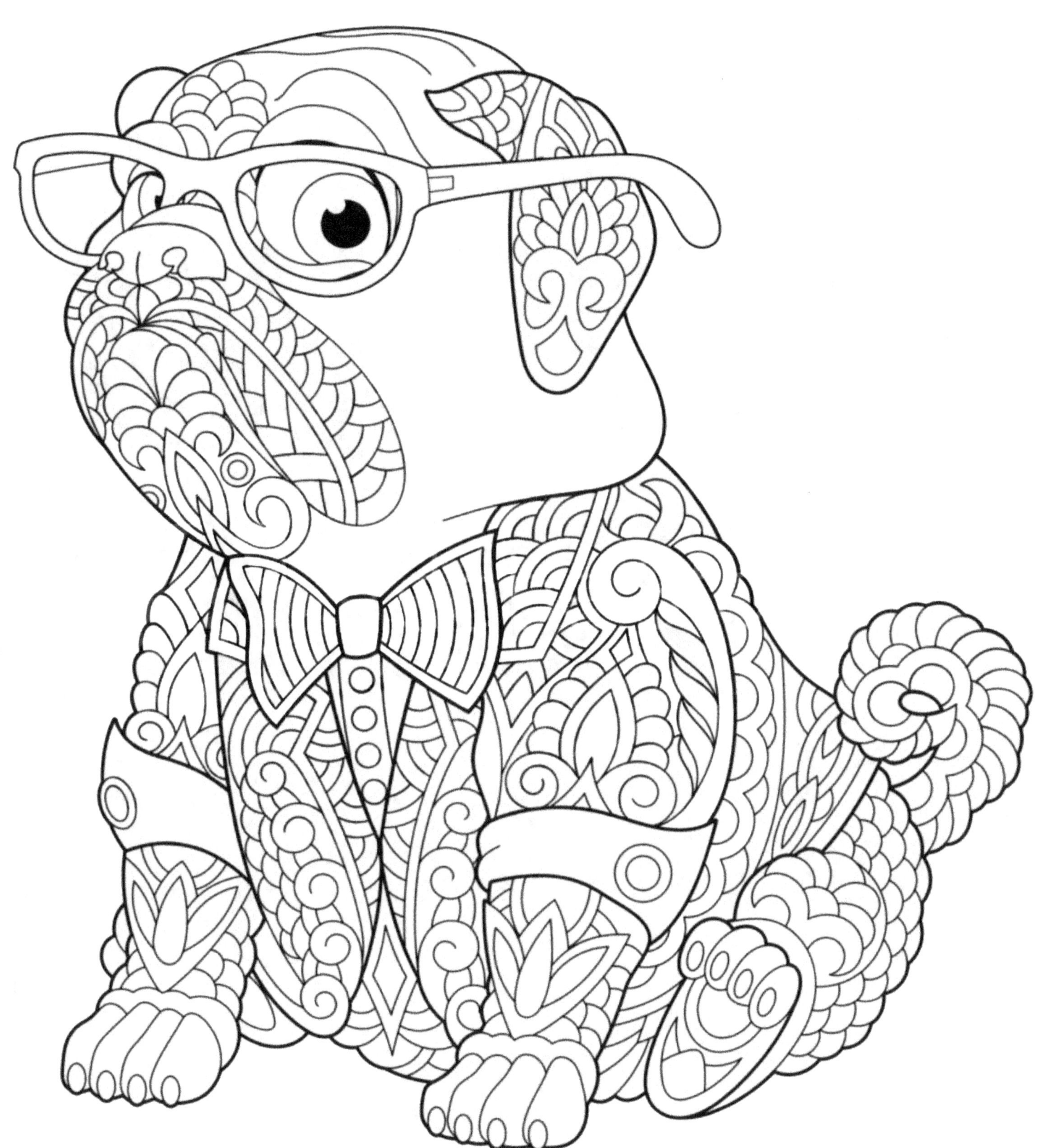

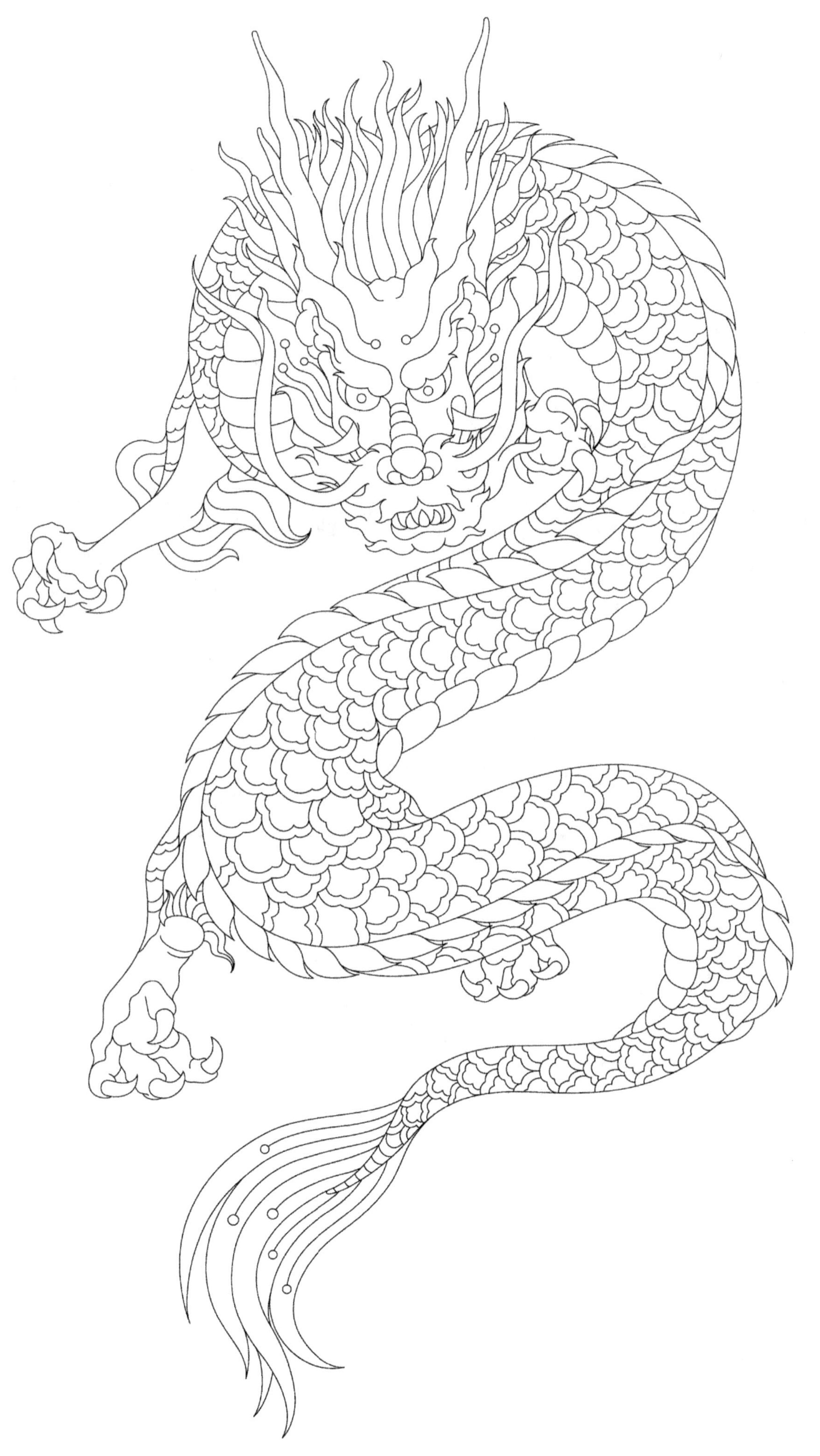

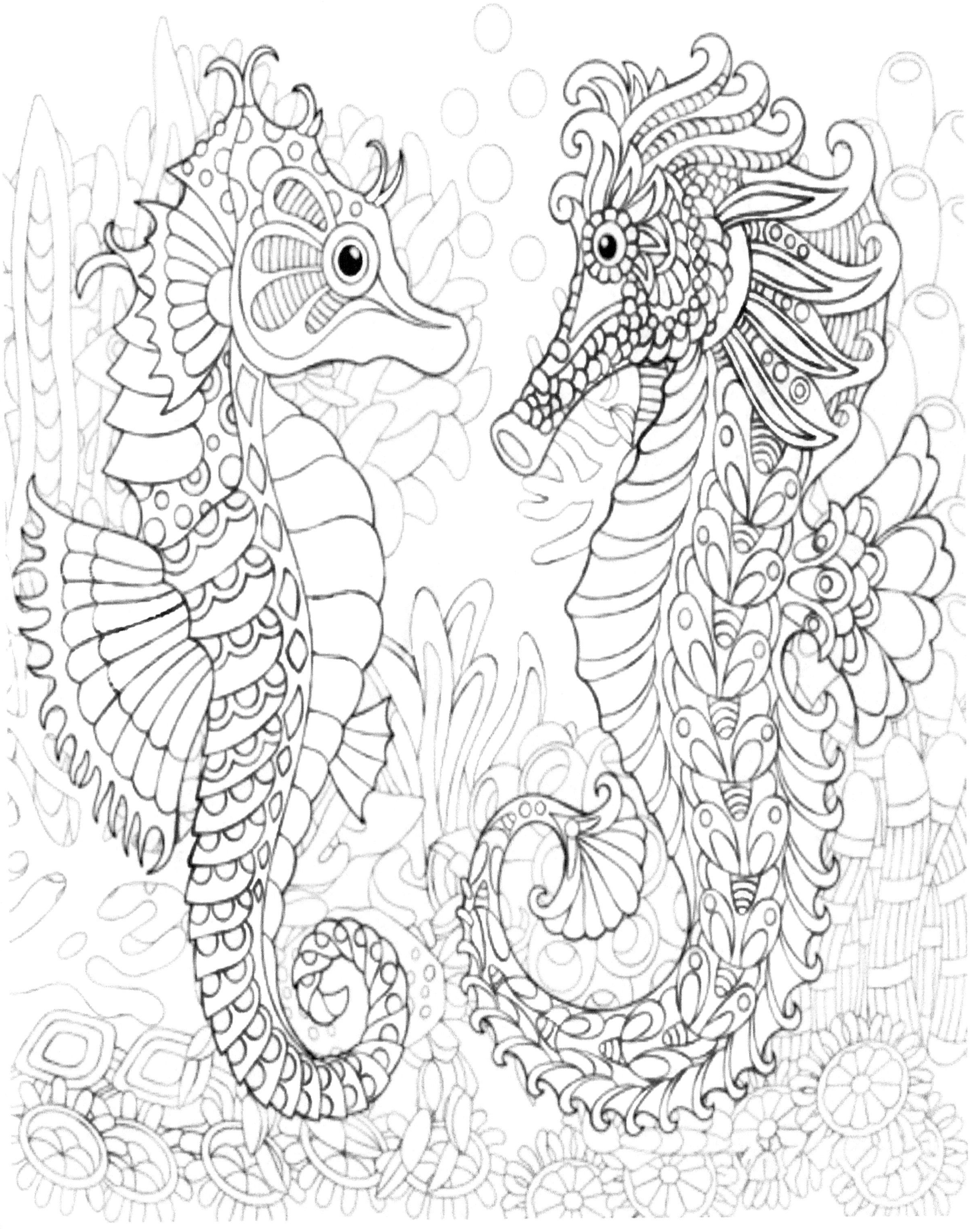

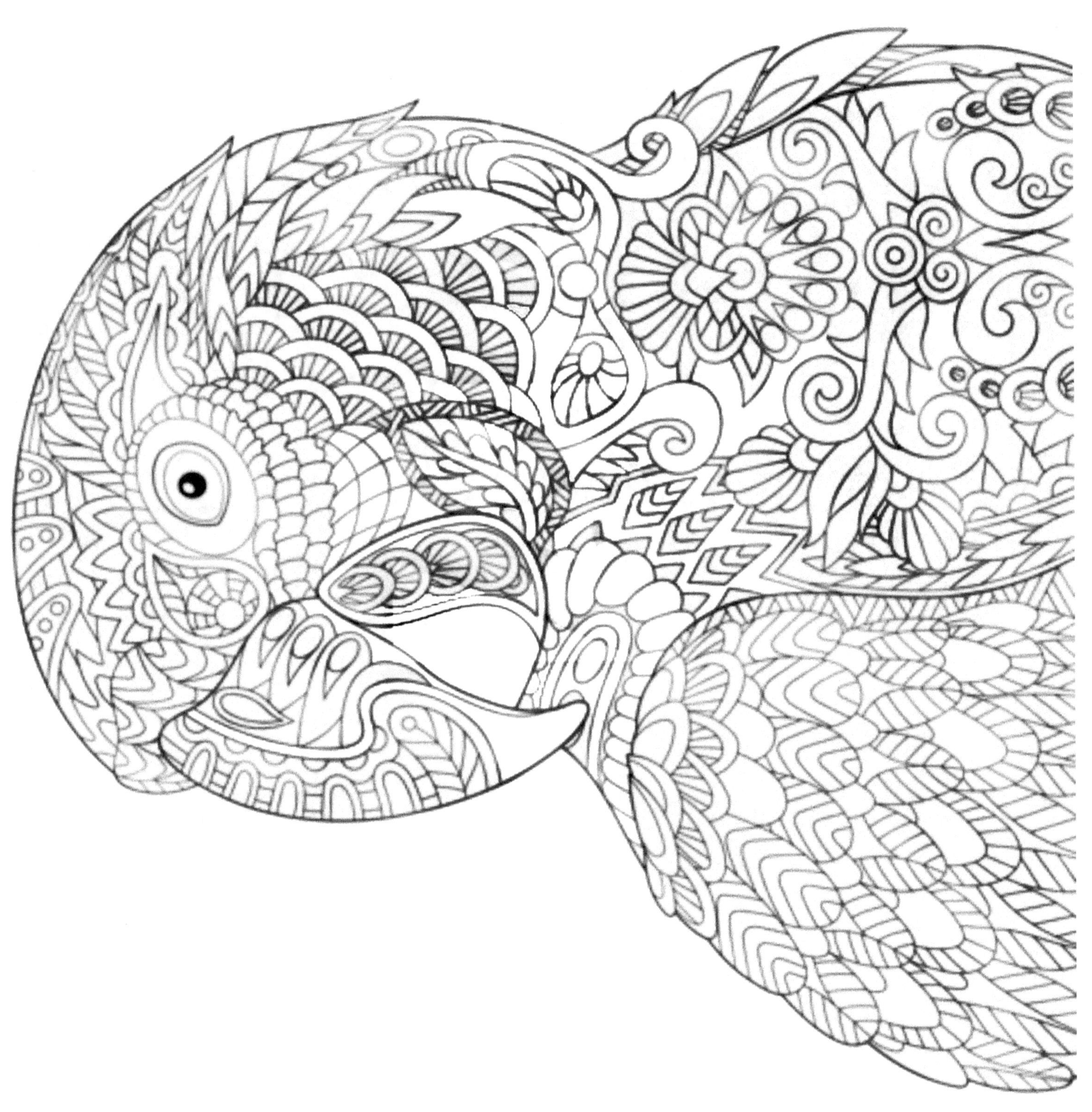

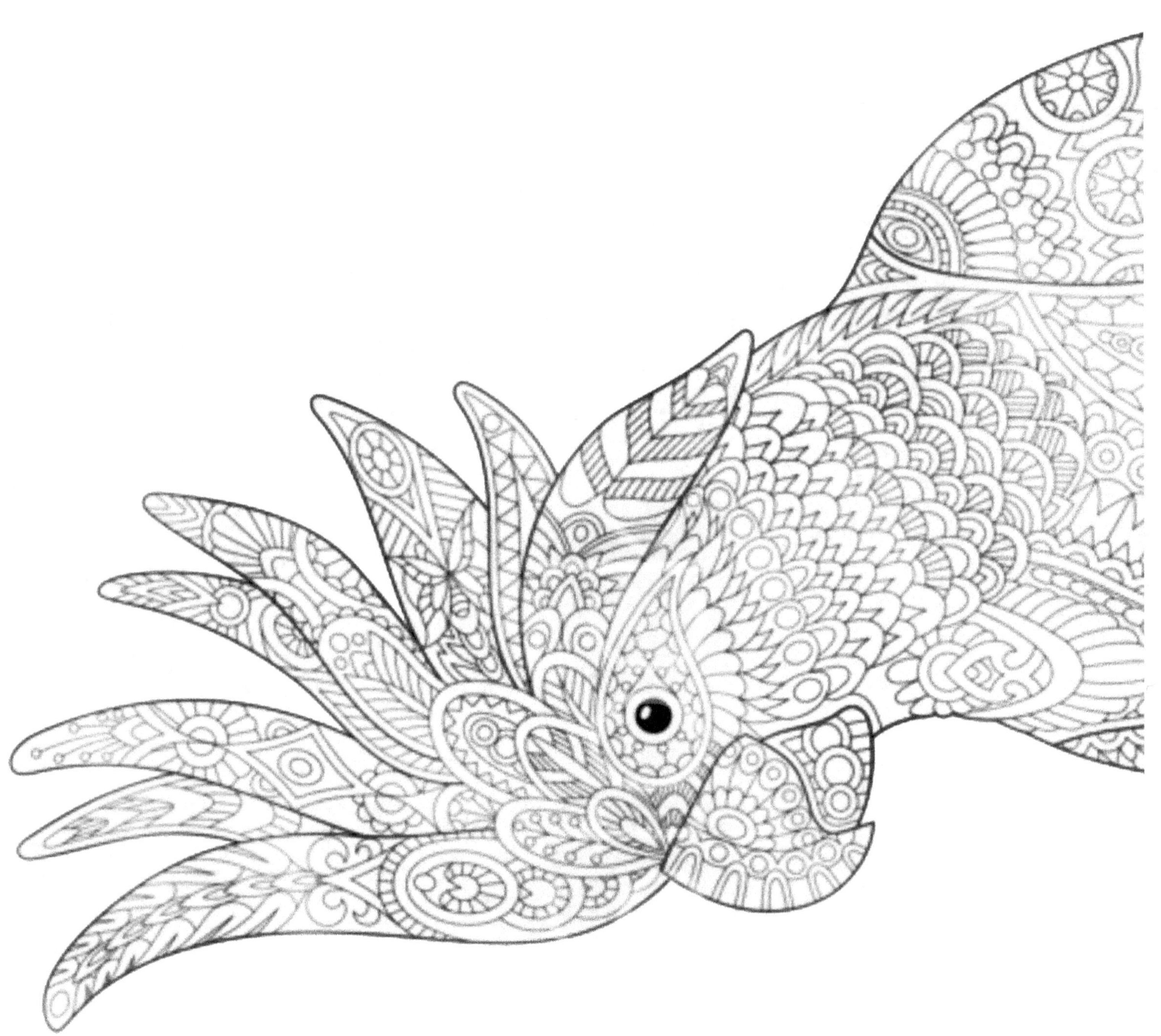

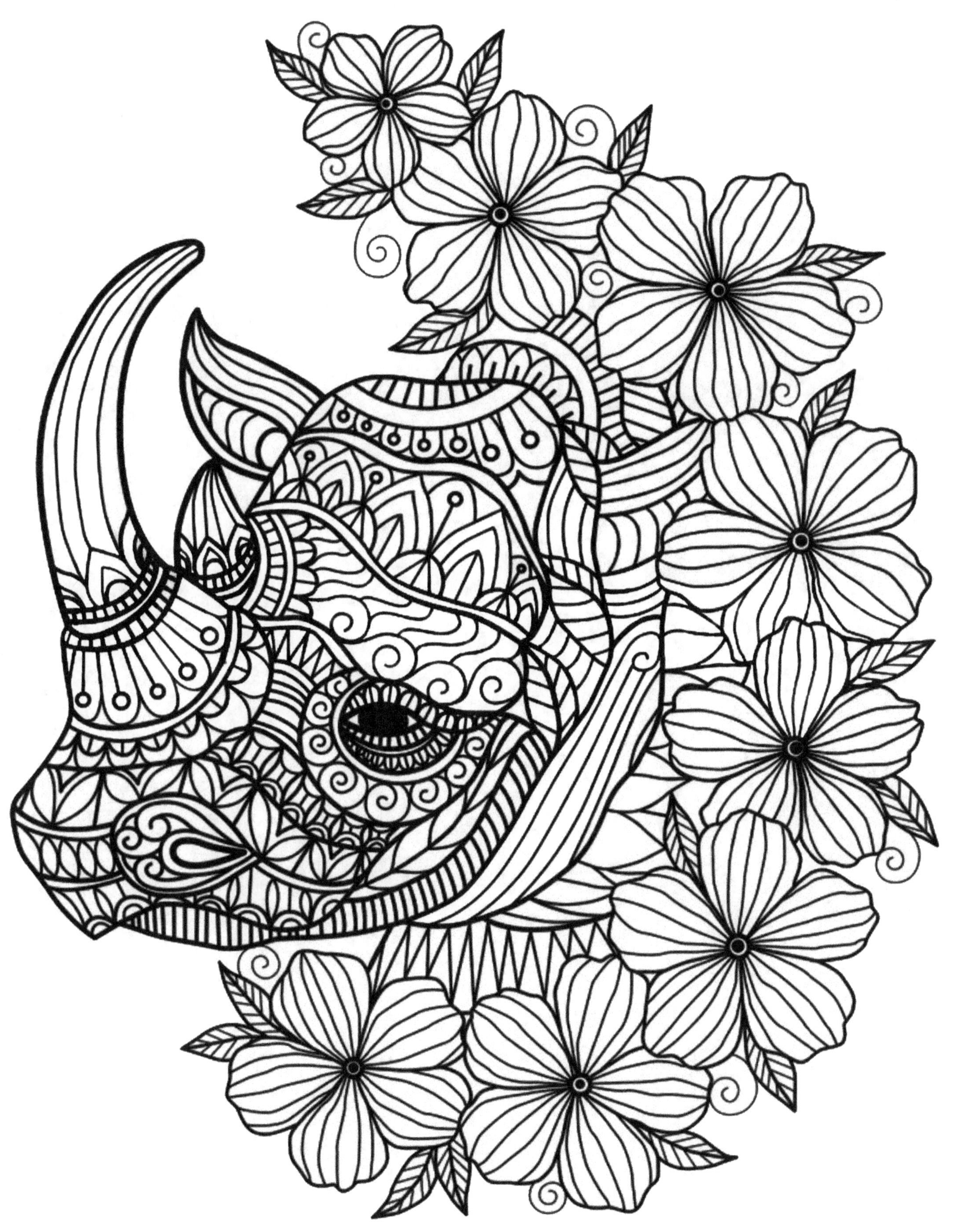

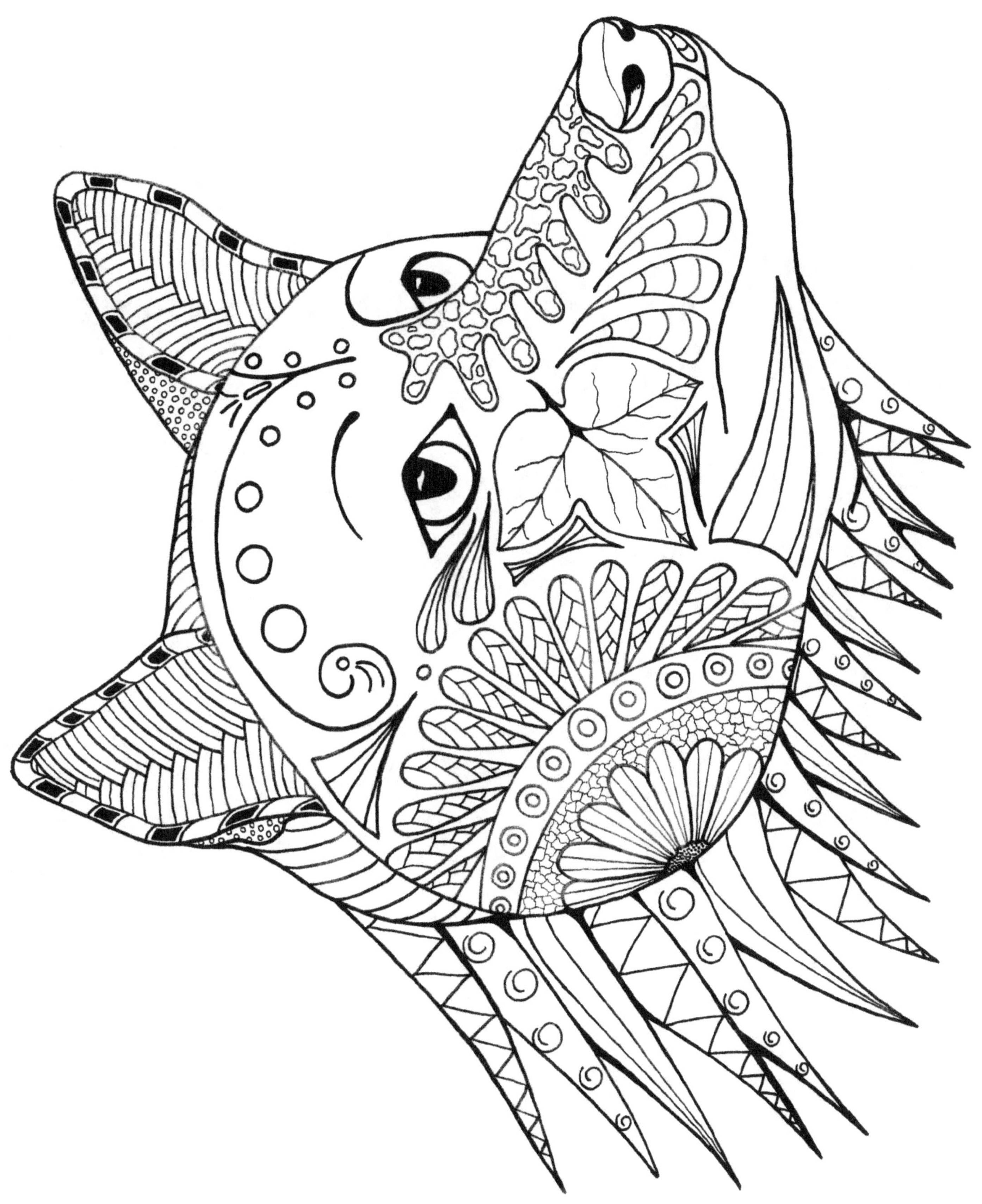

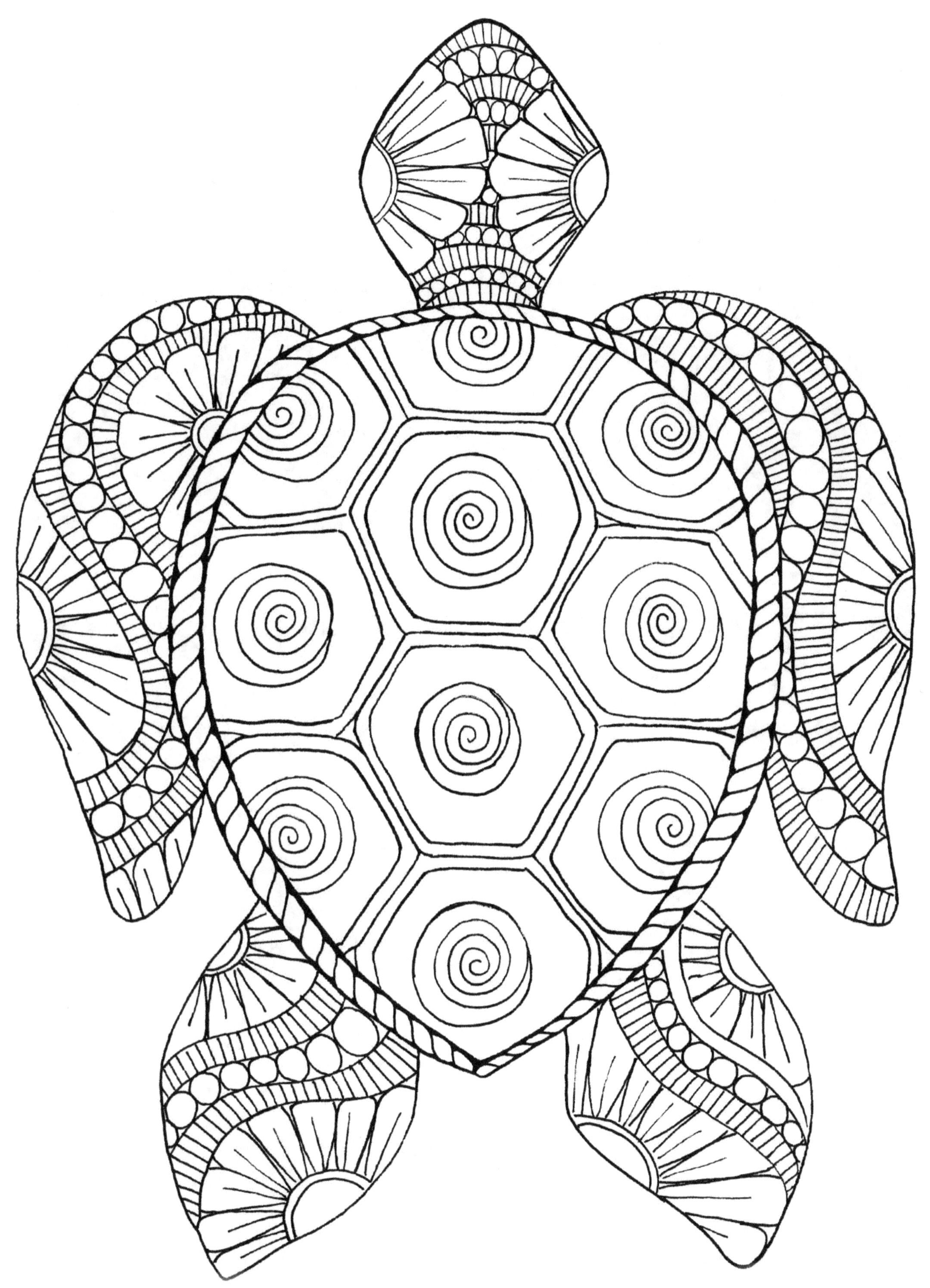

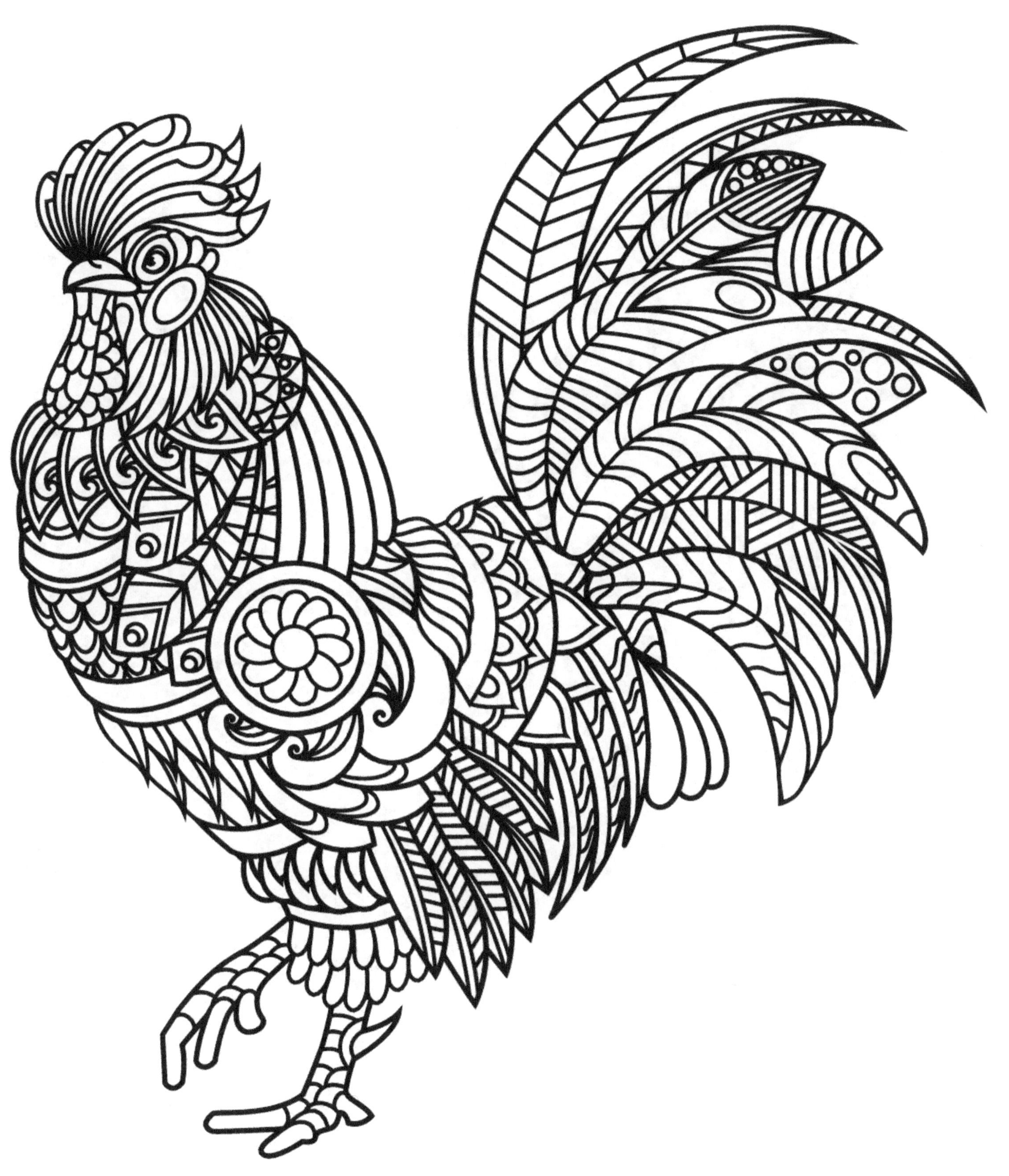

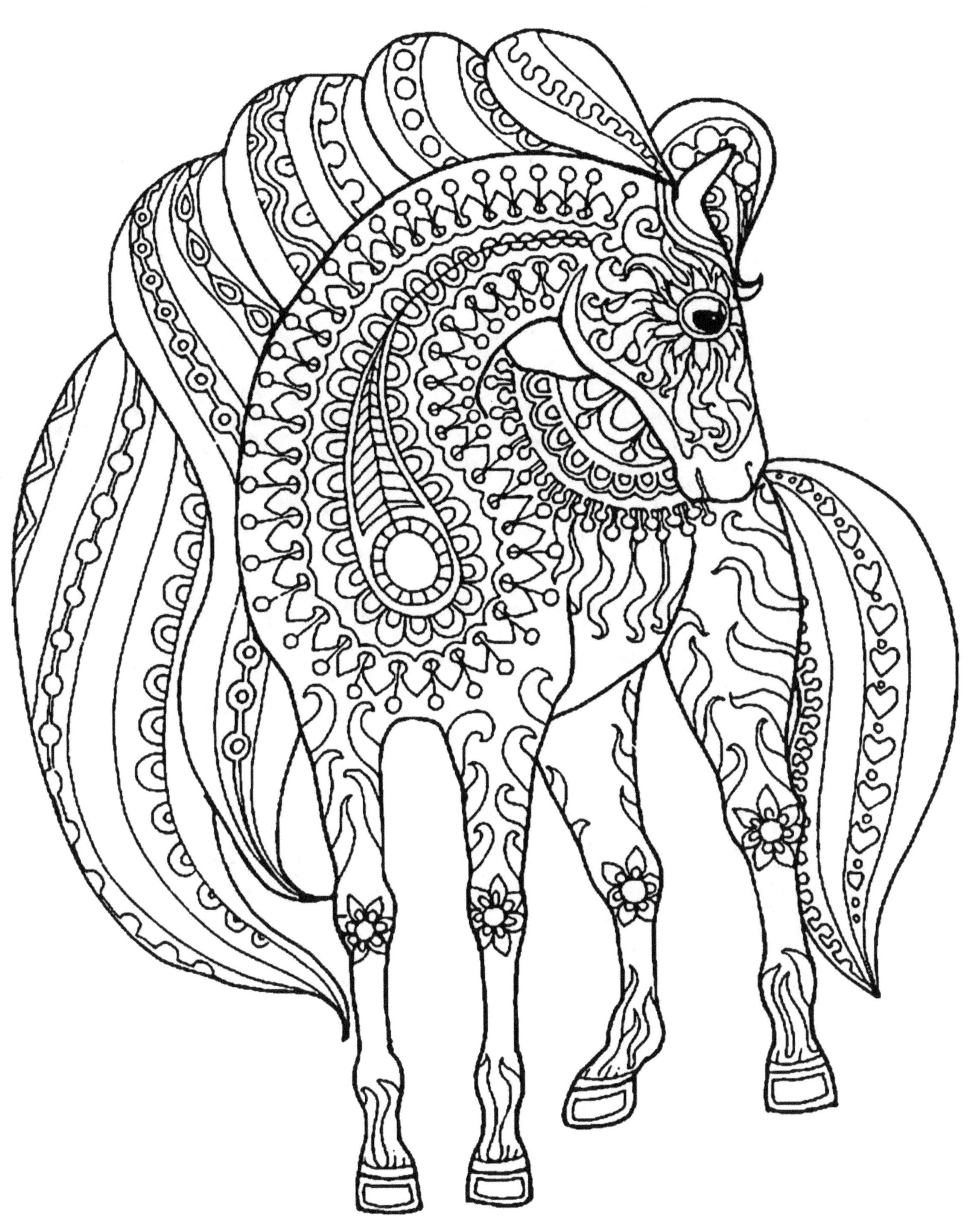

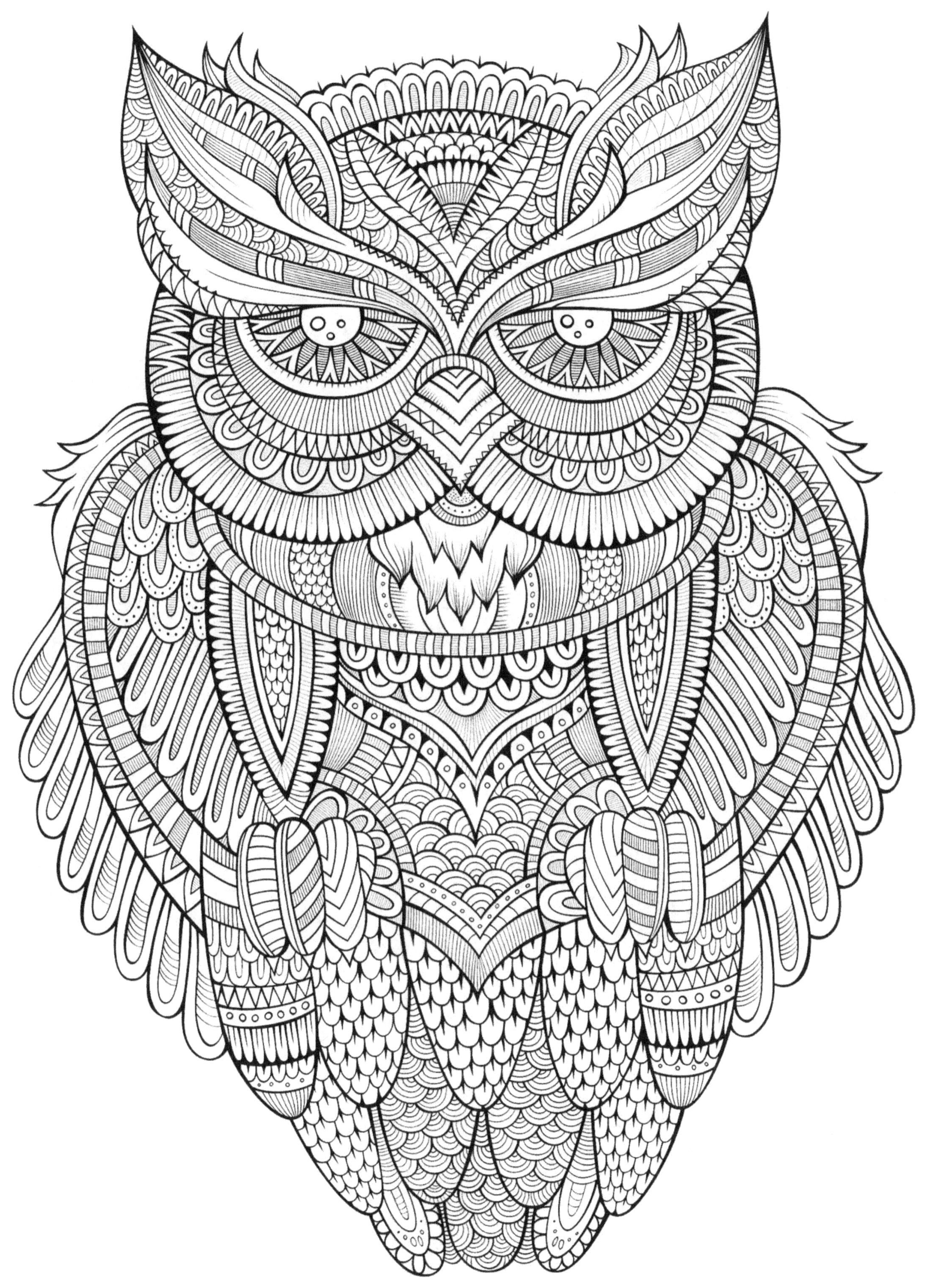

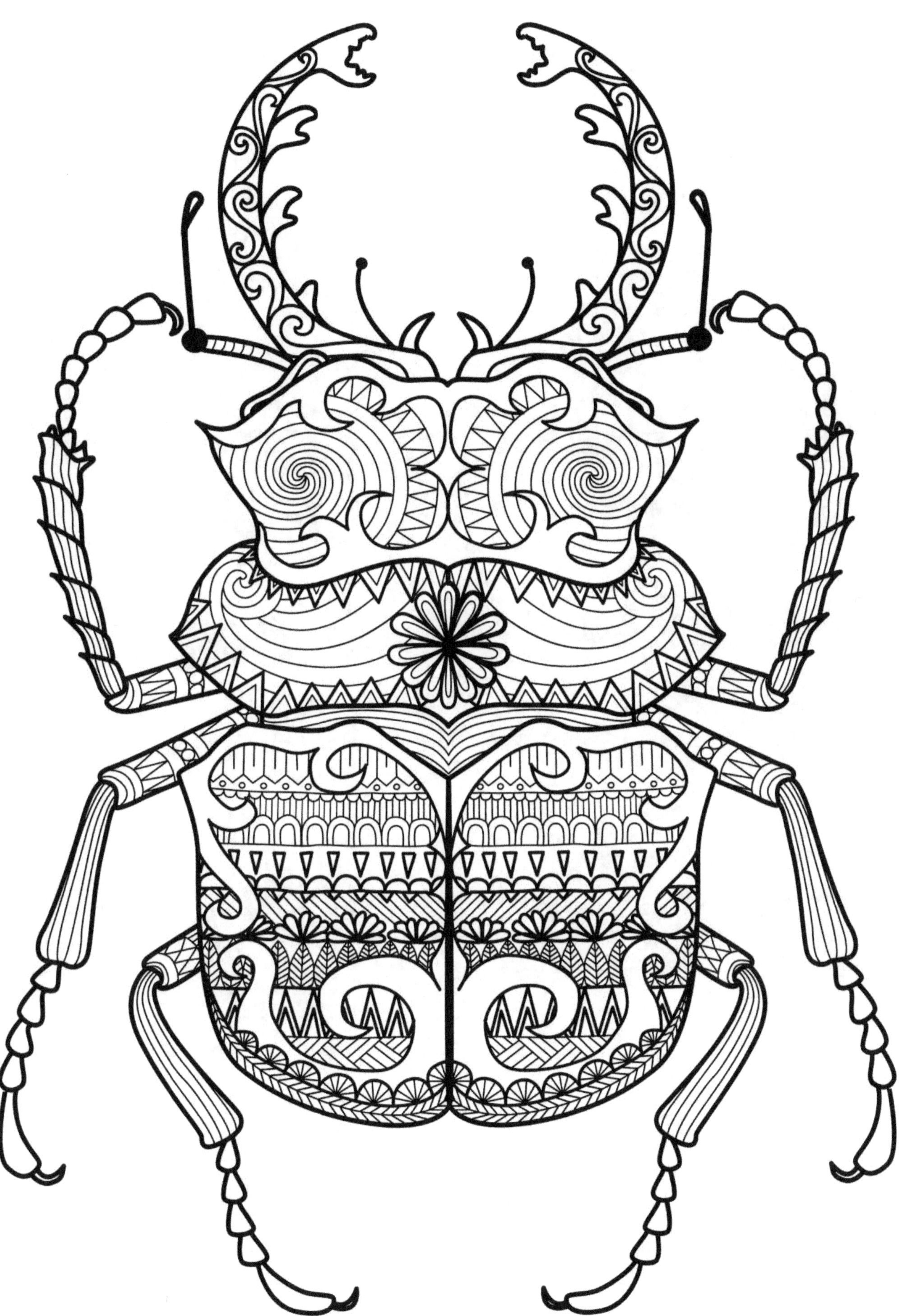

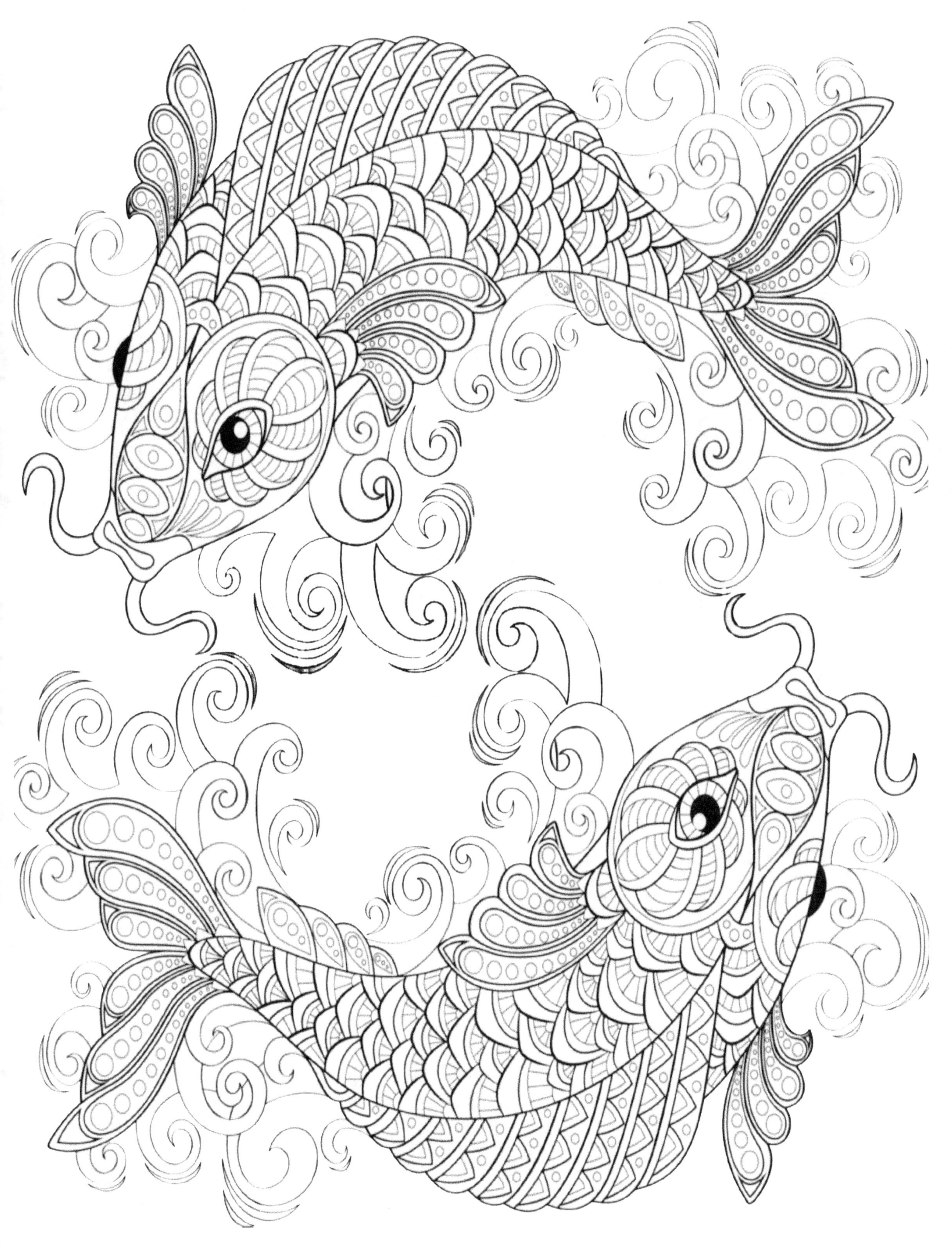

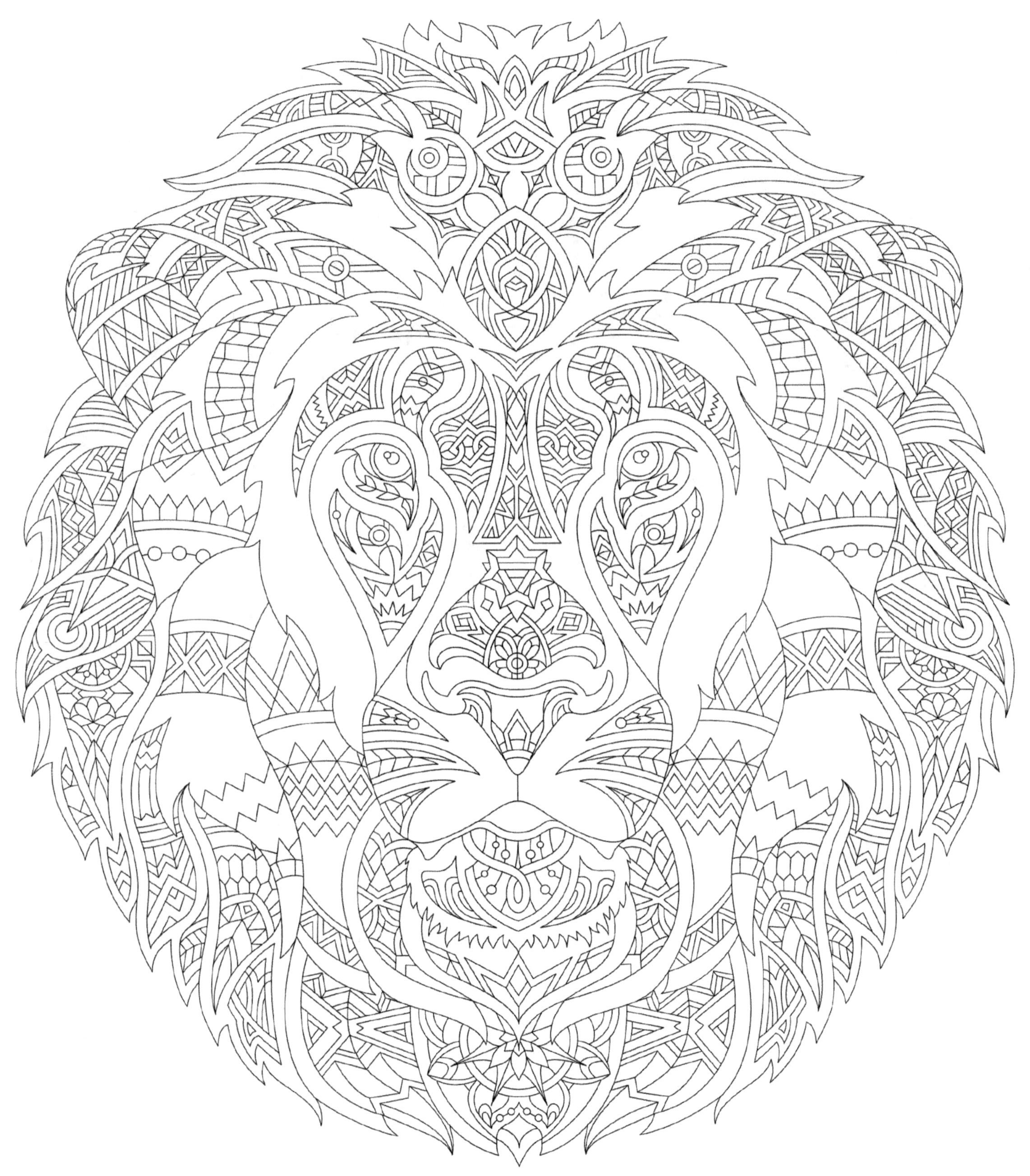

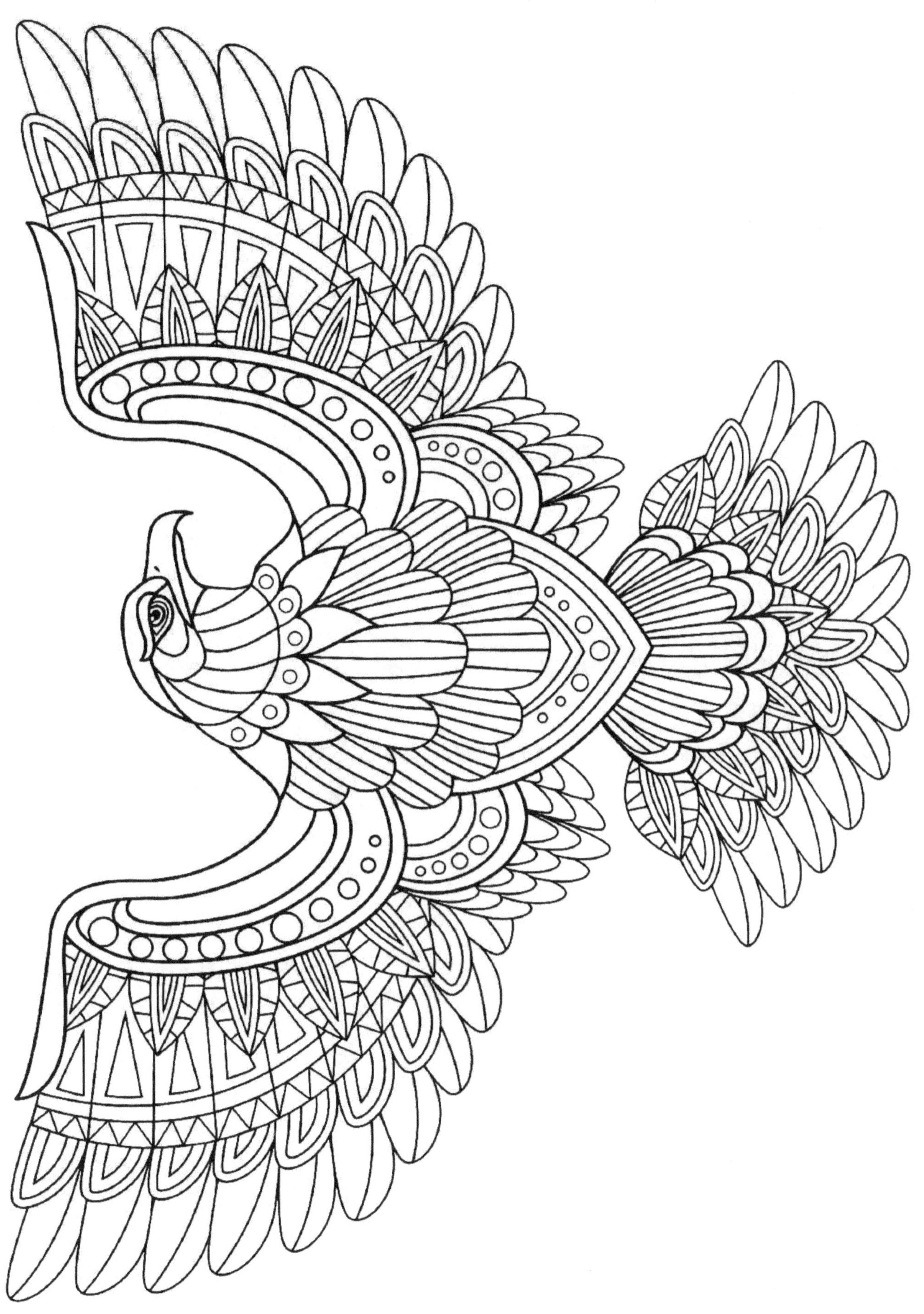

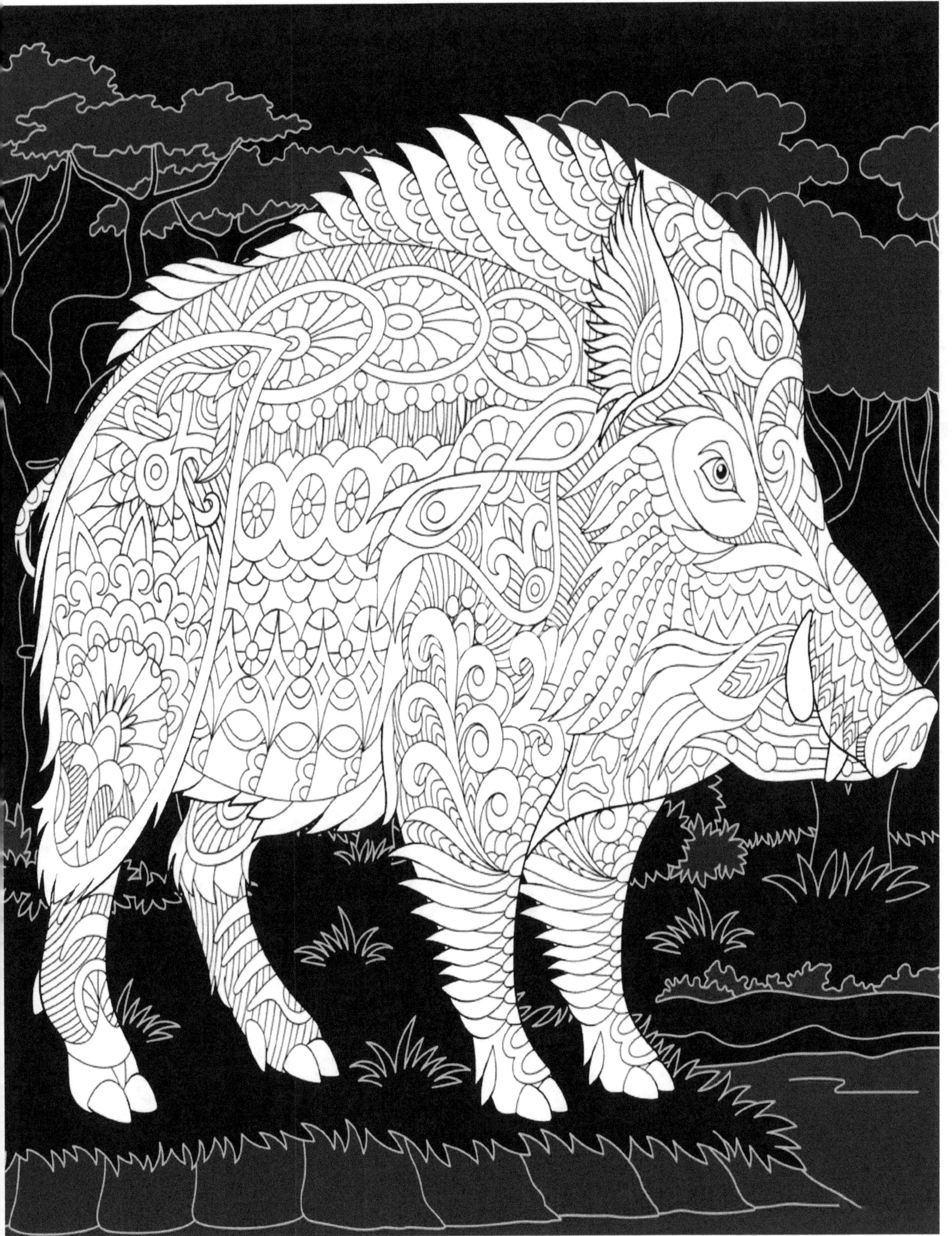

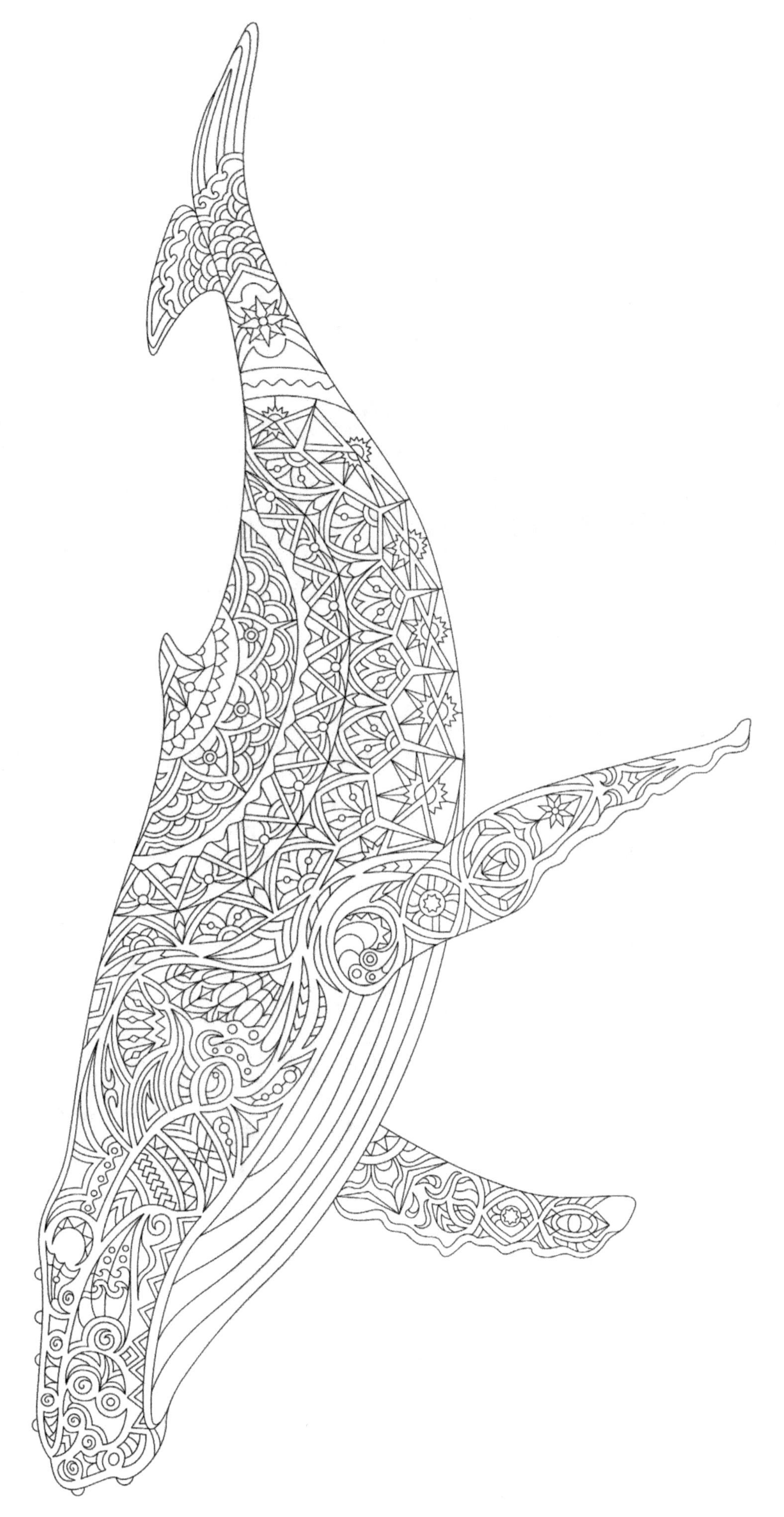

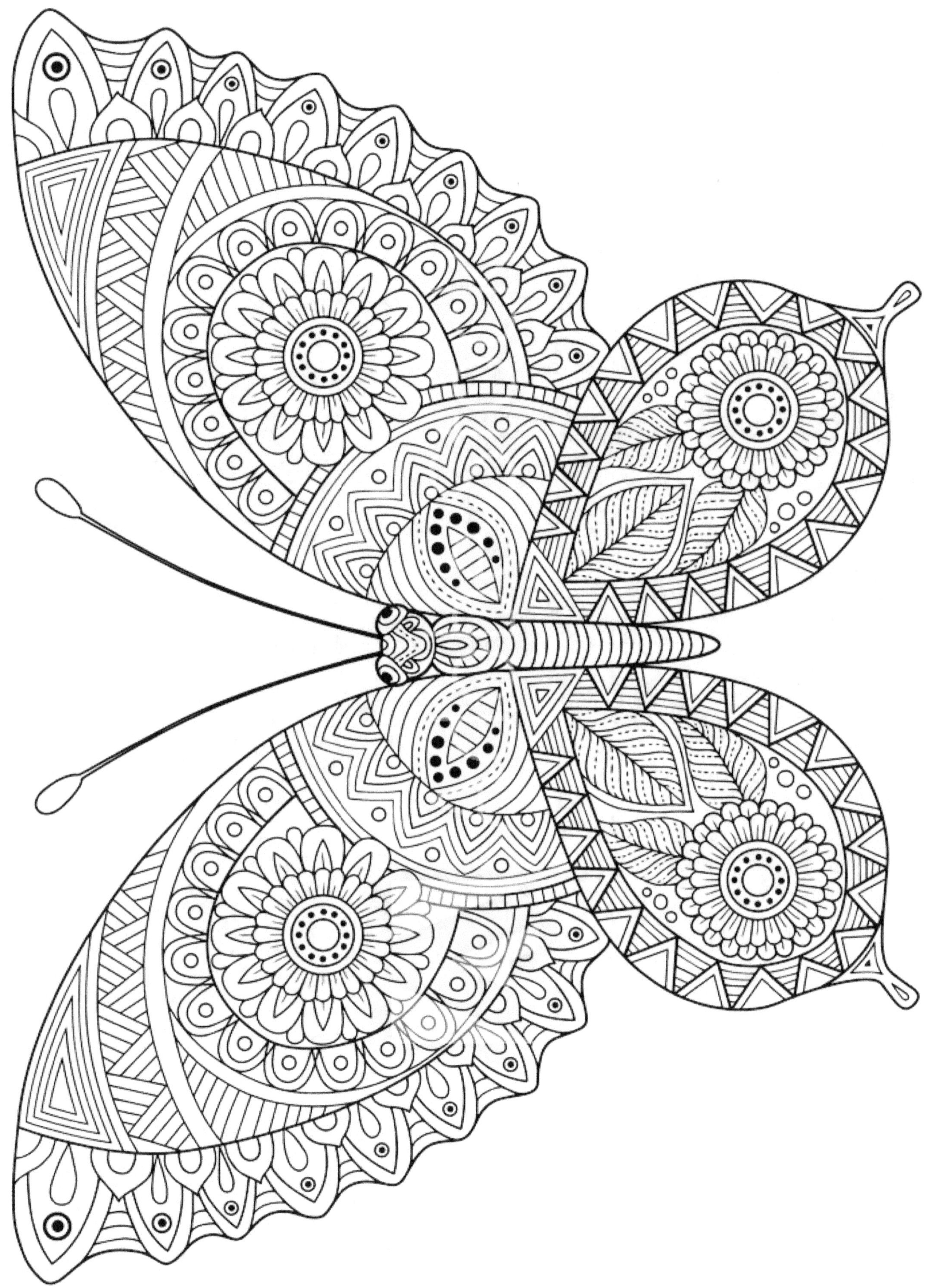

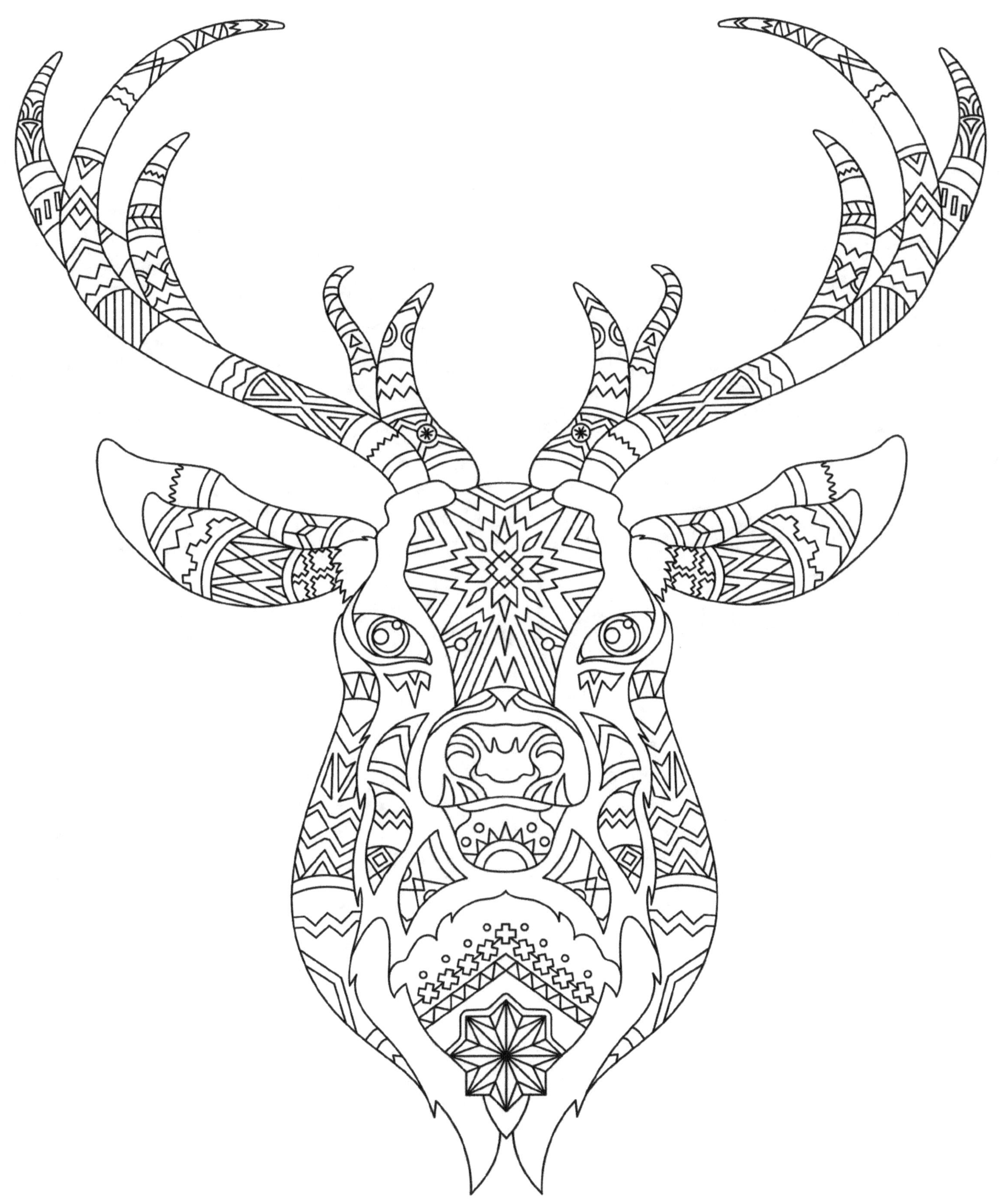

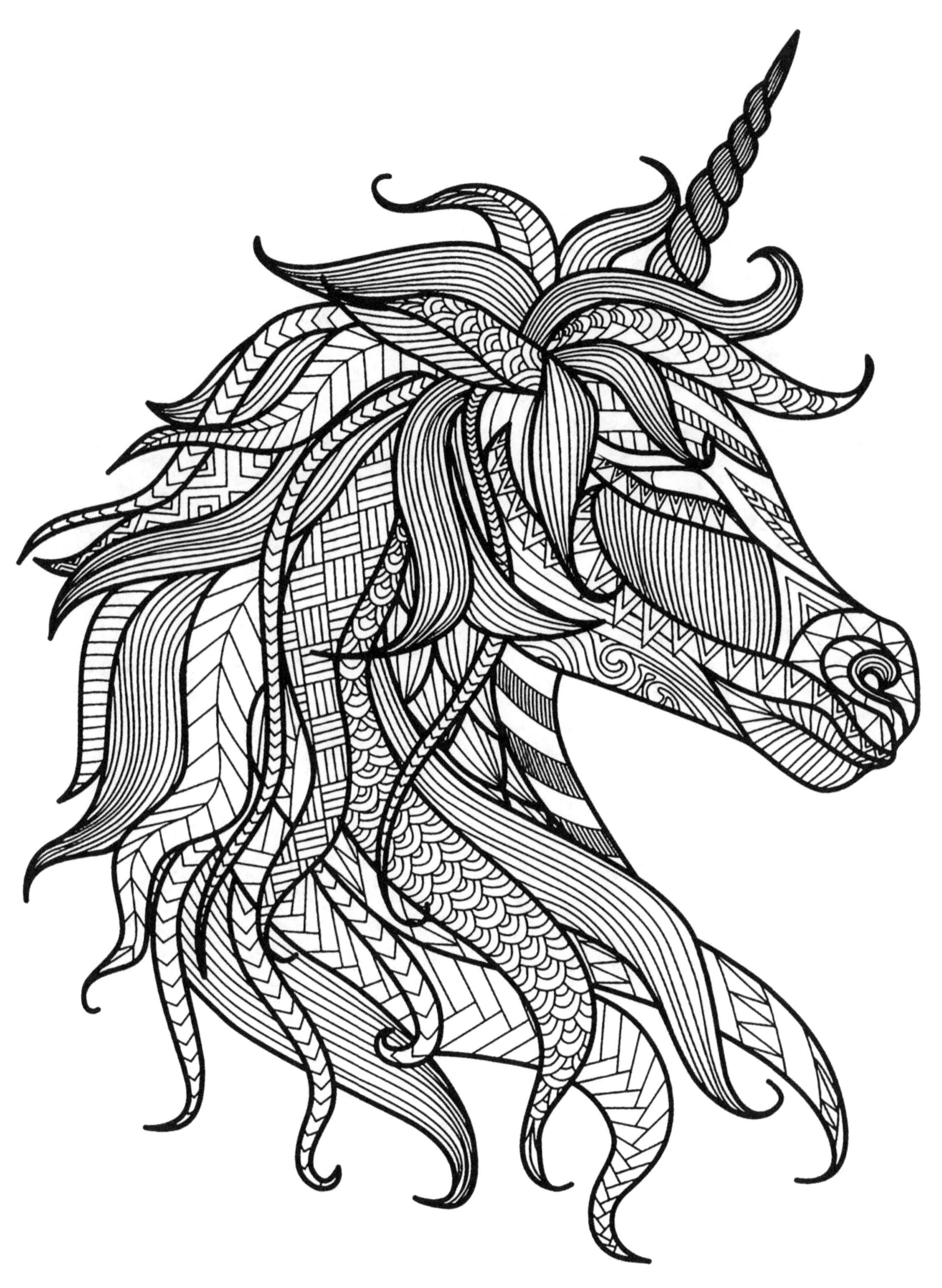

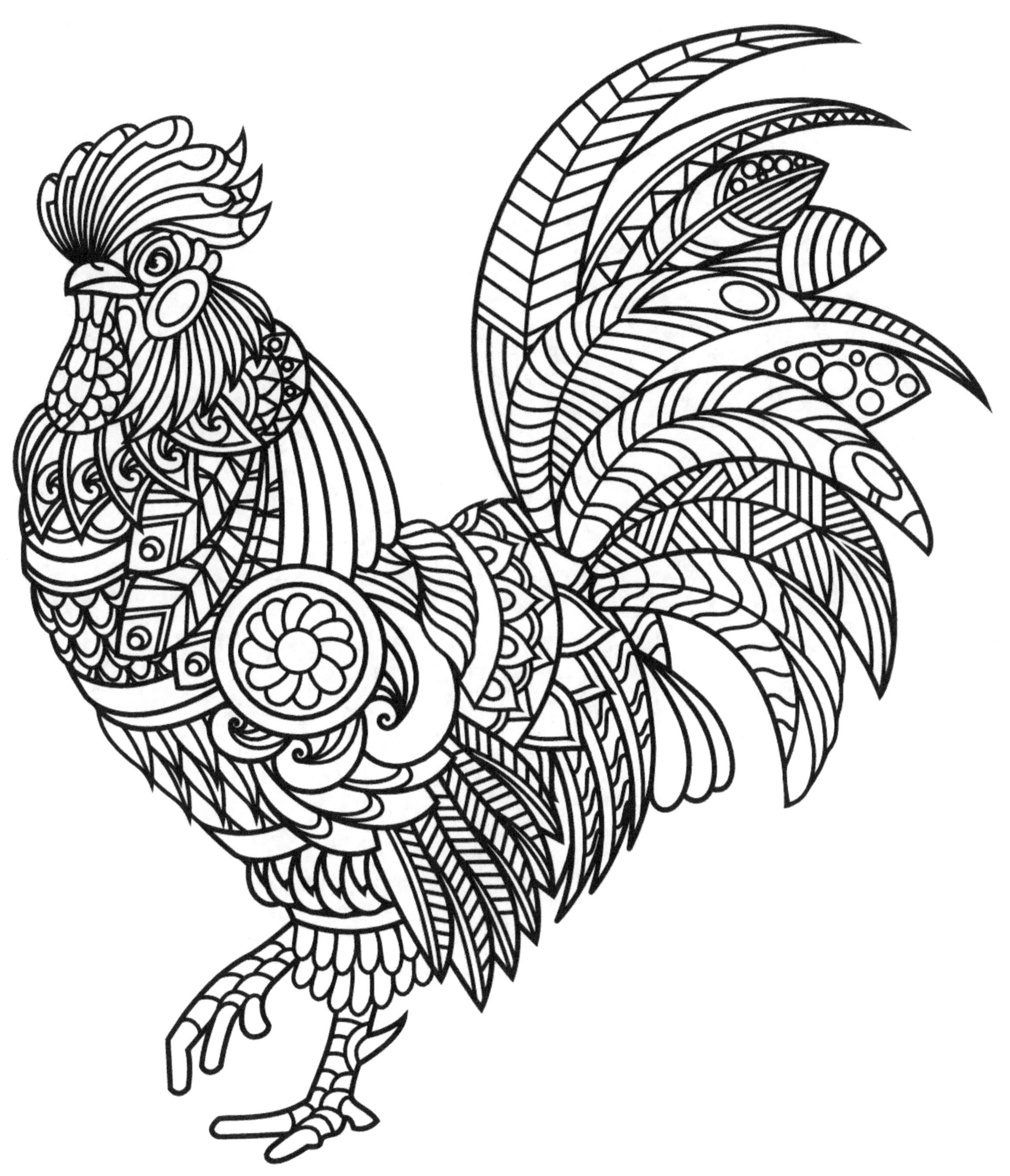

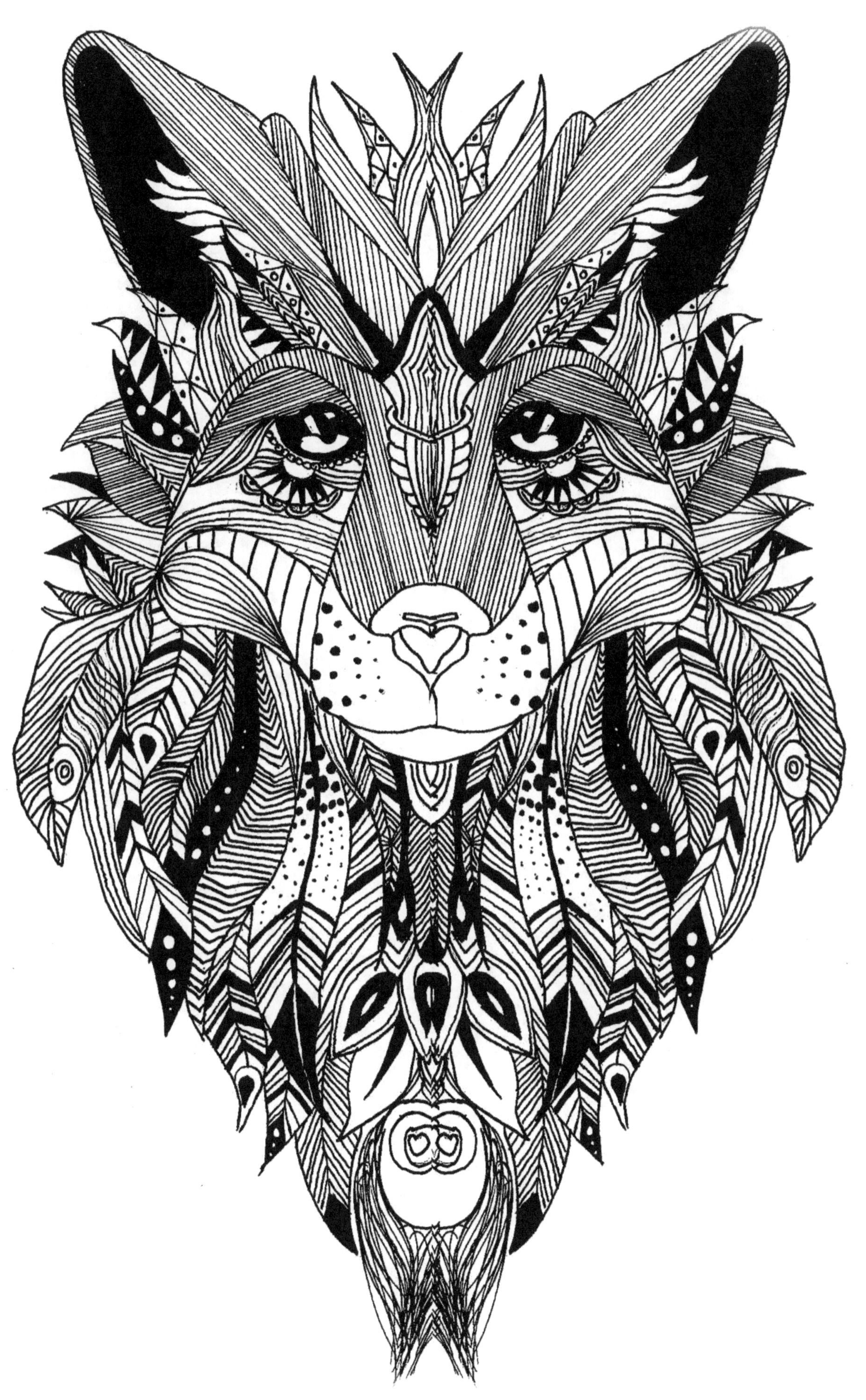

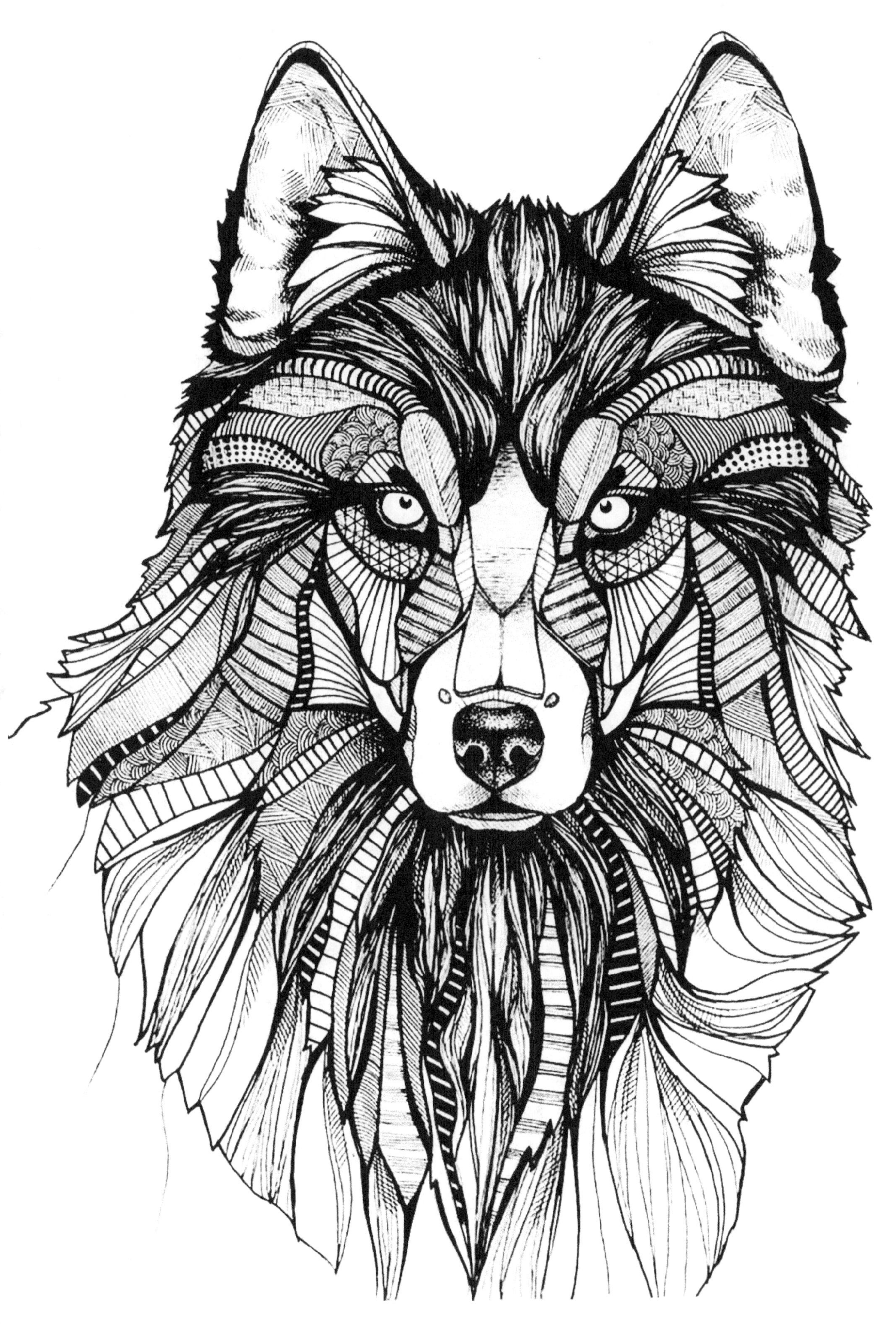

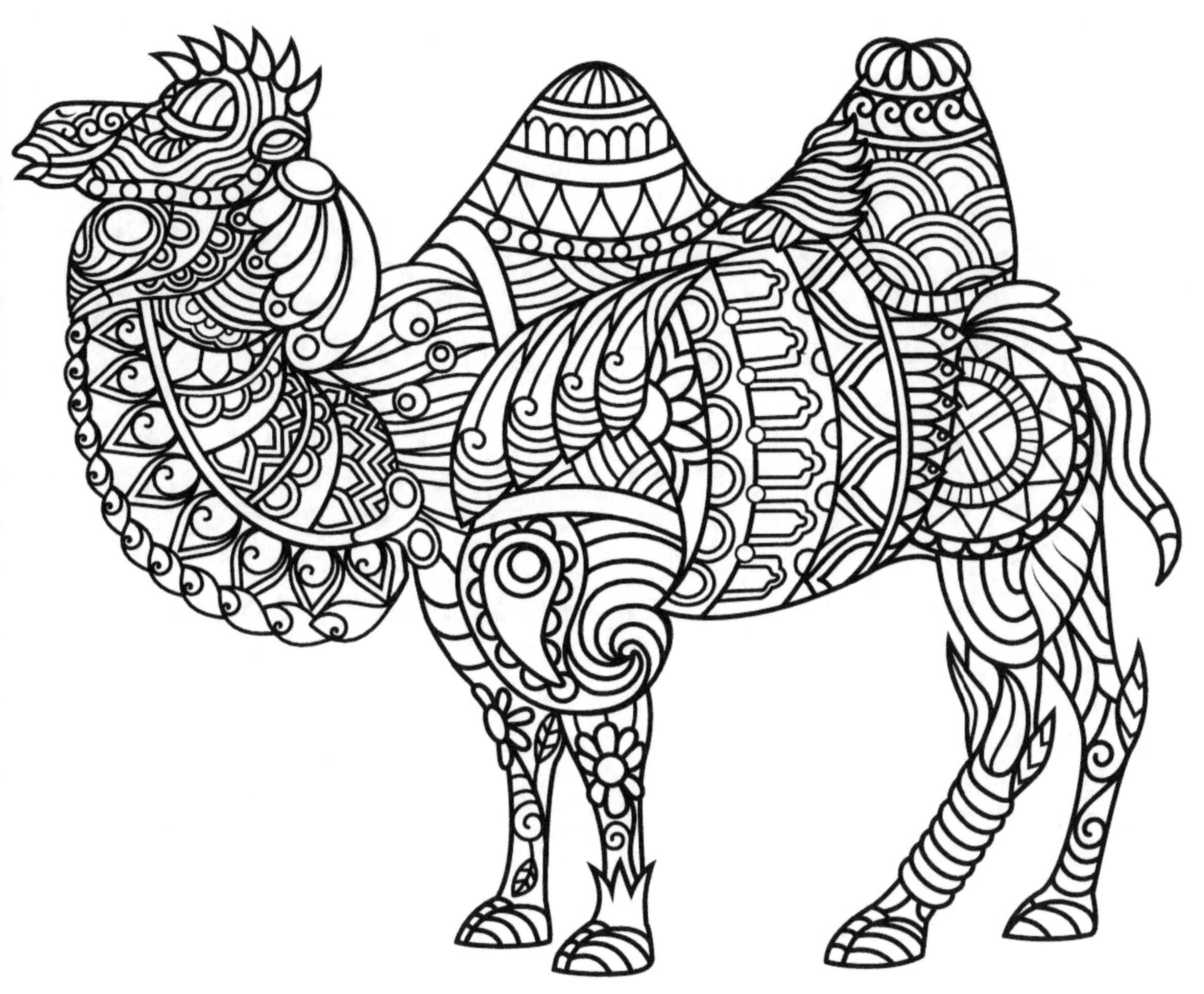

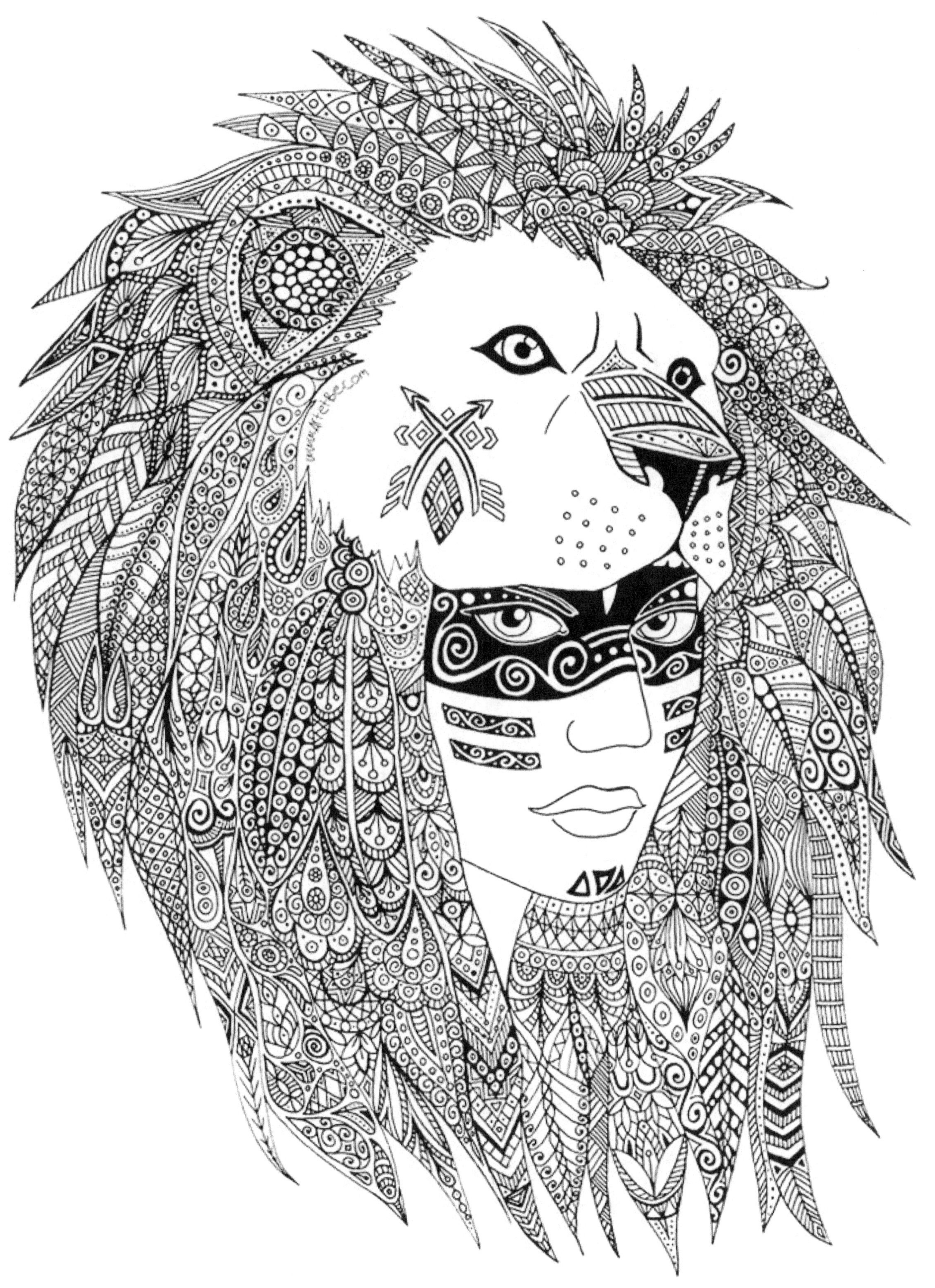

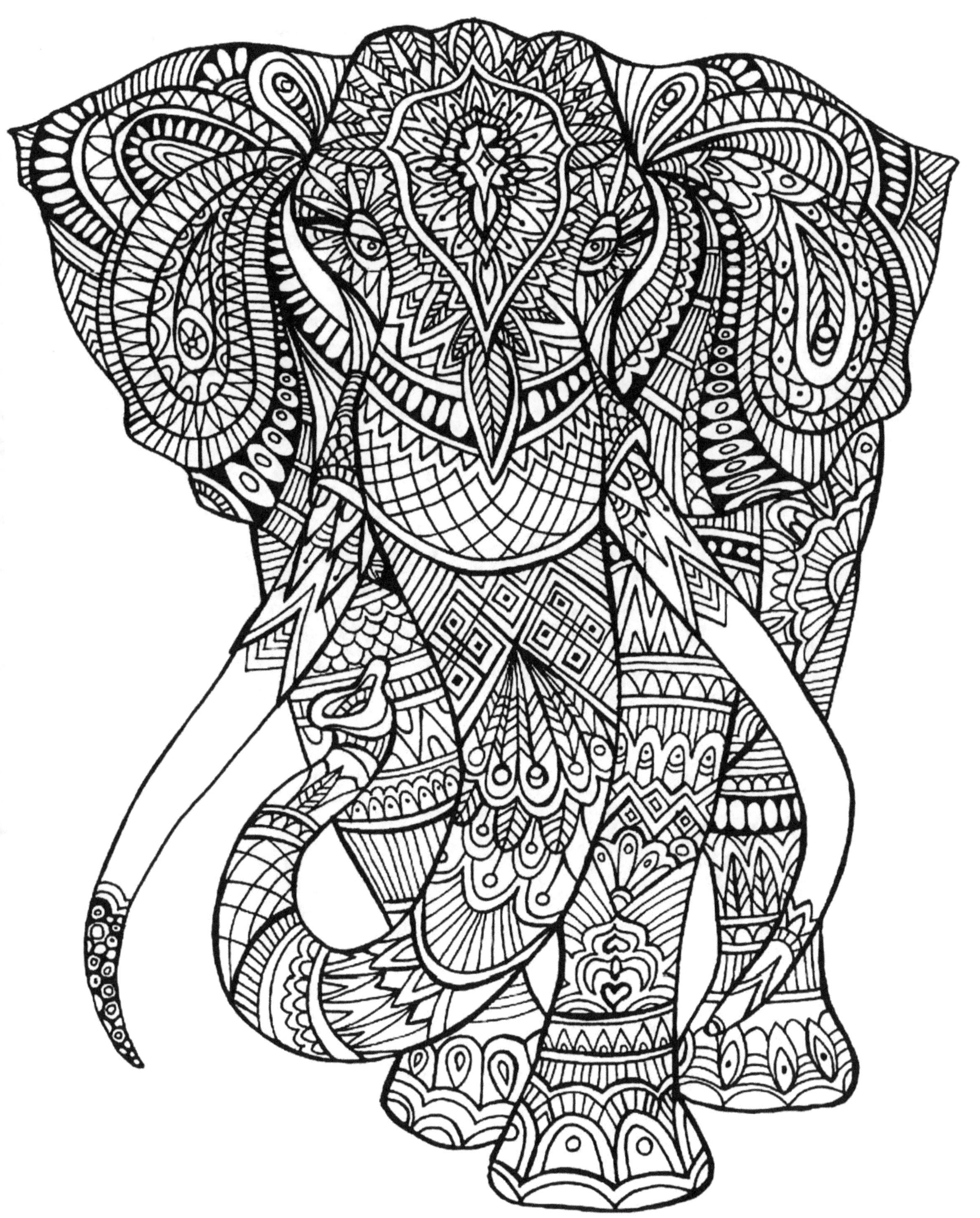

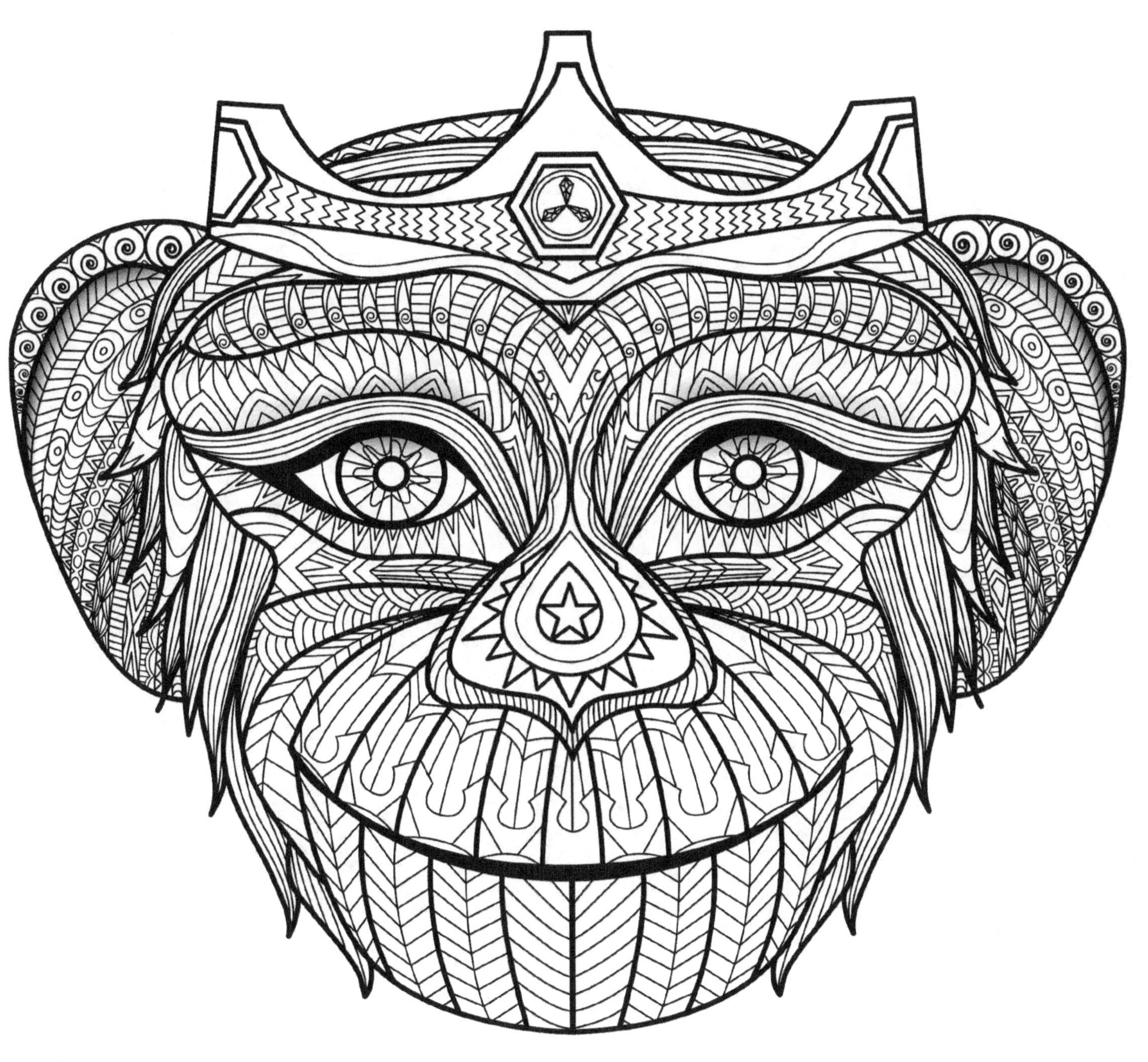

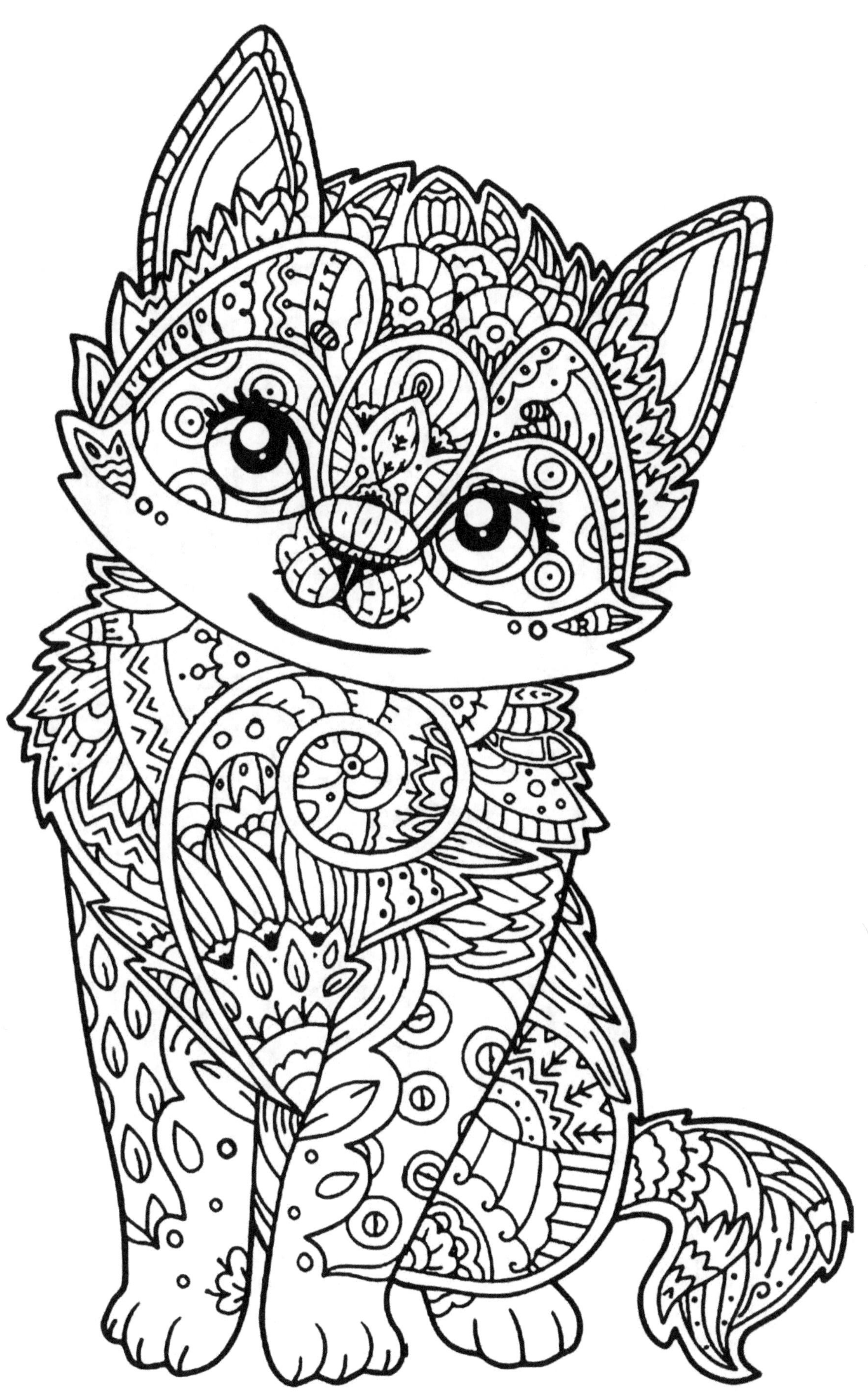

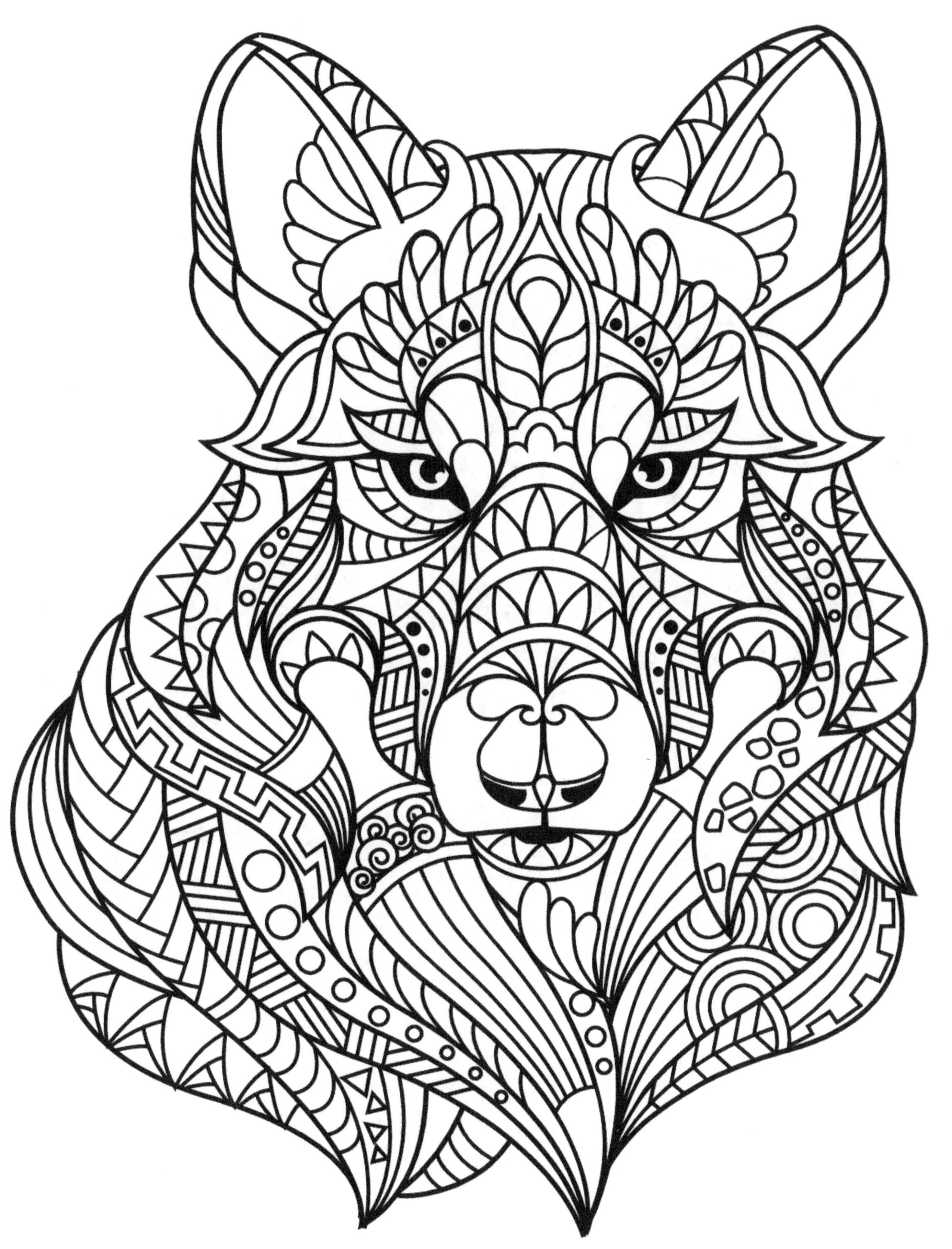

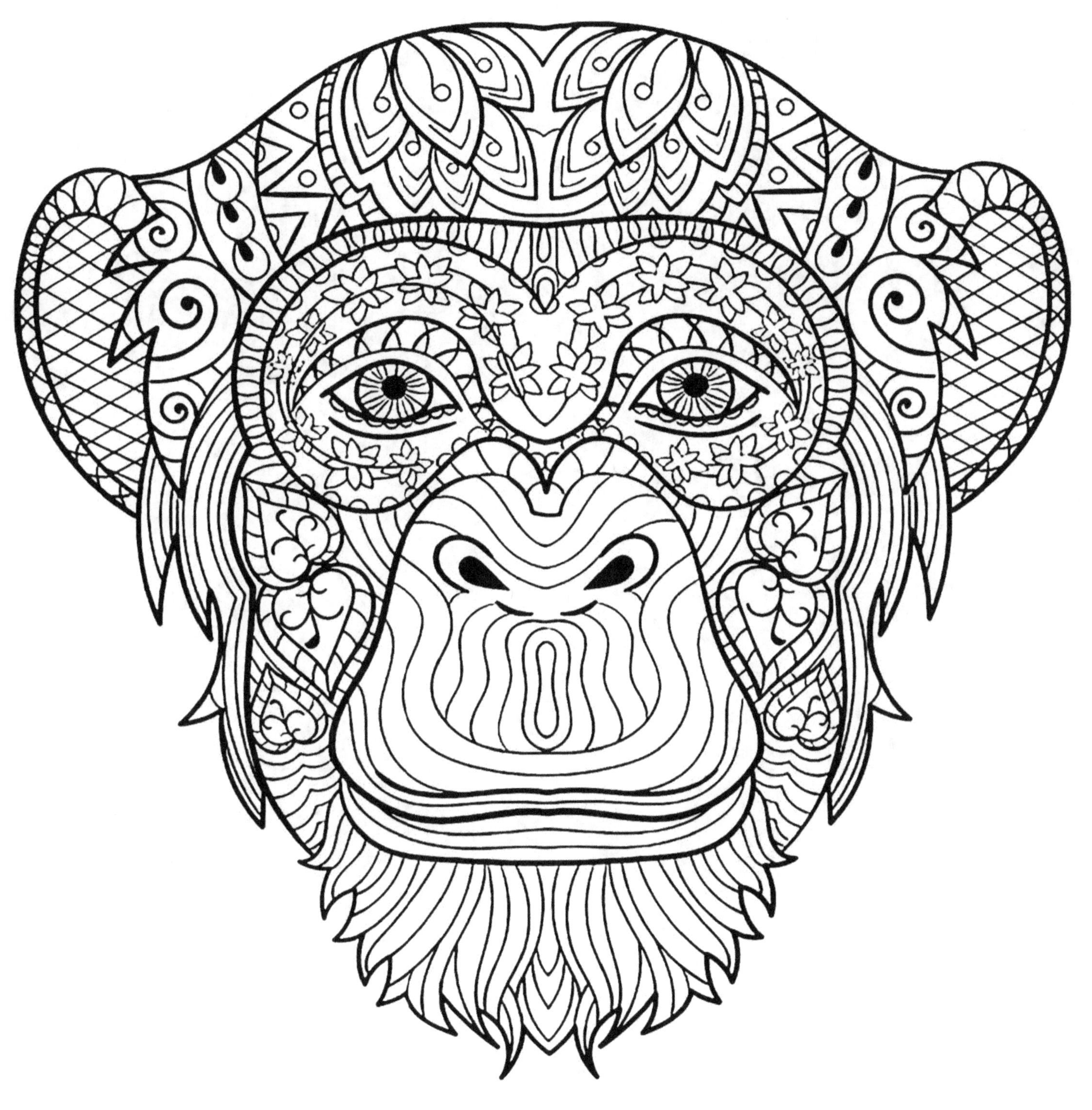

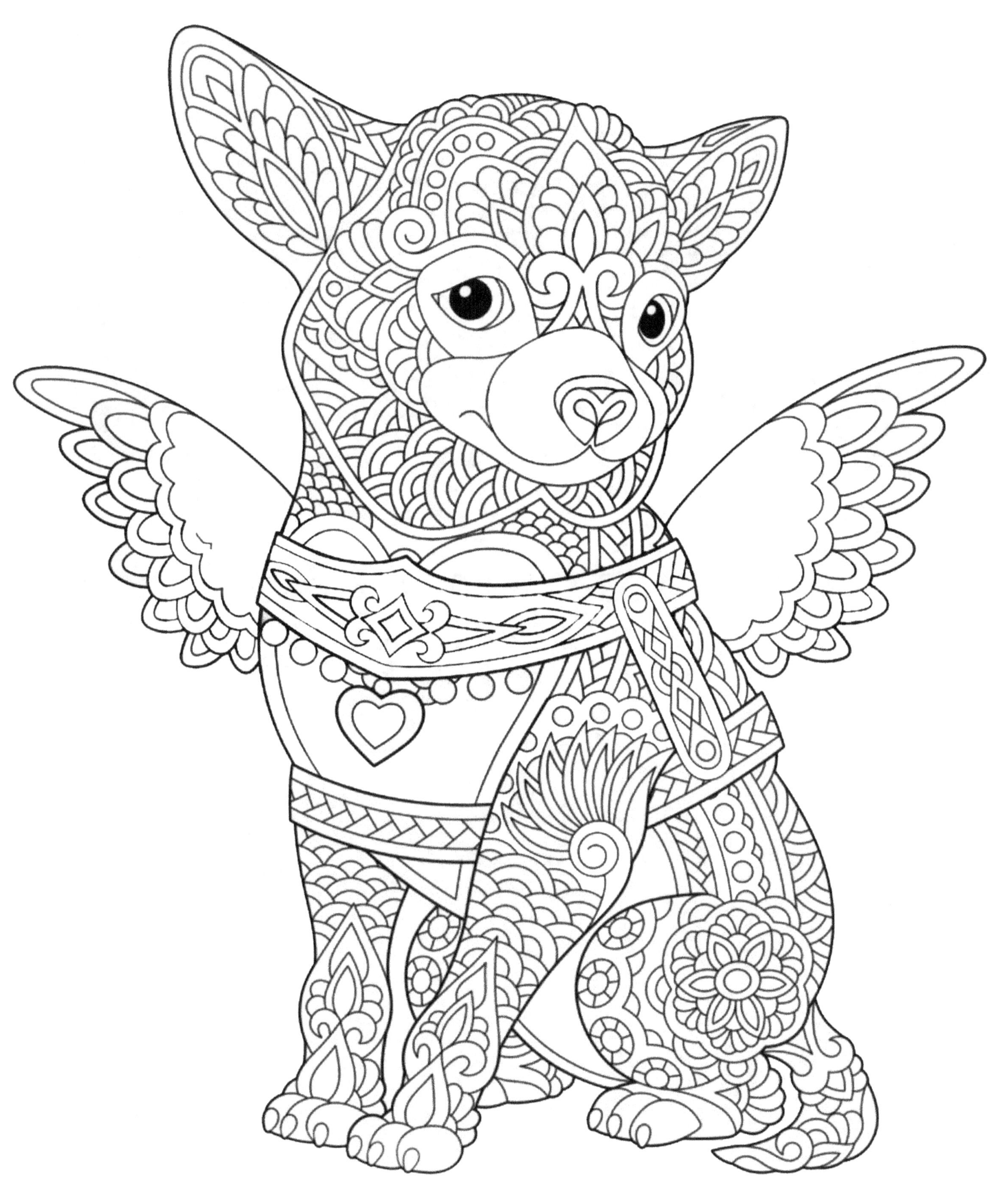

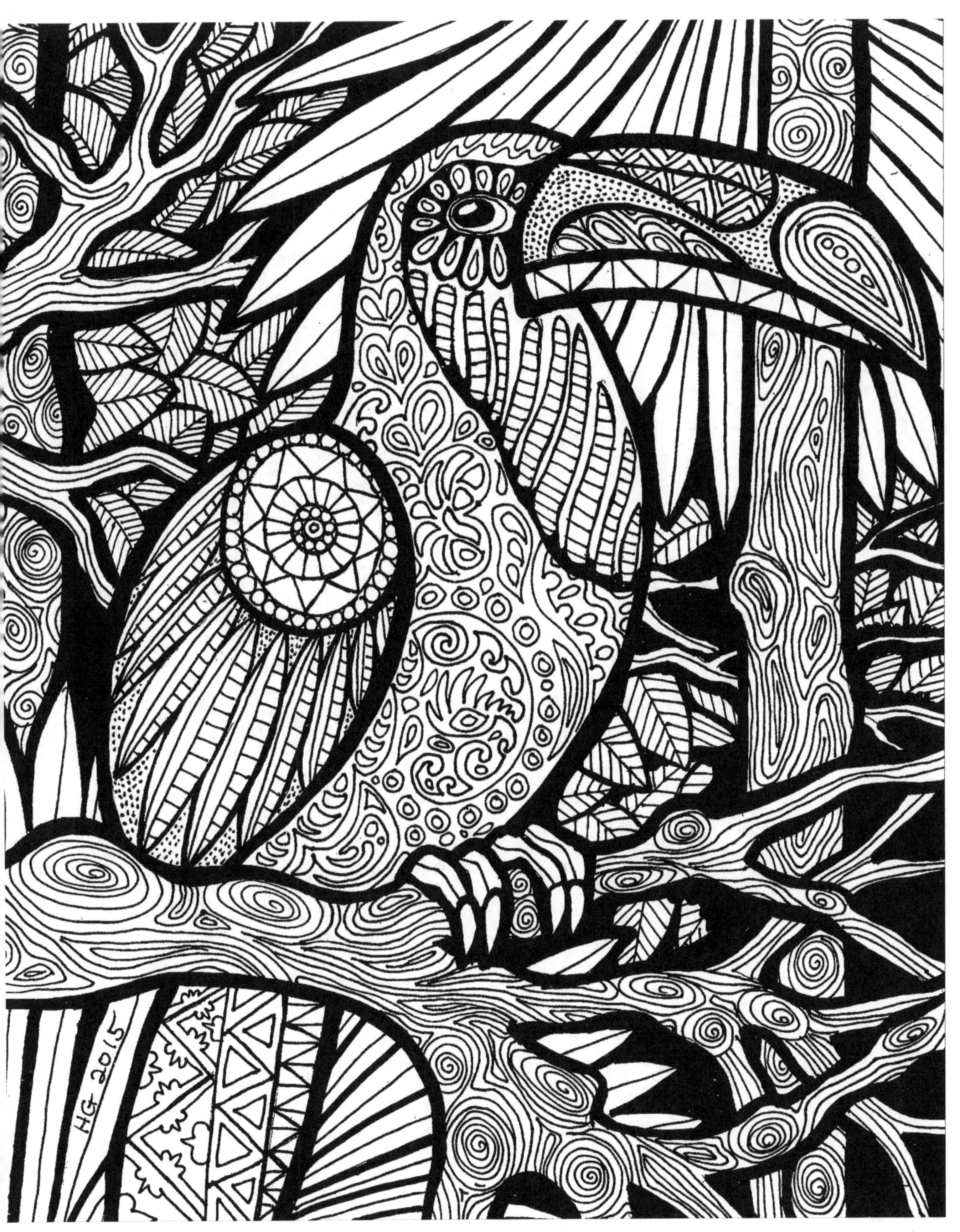
HG - 2015

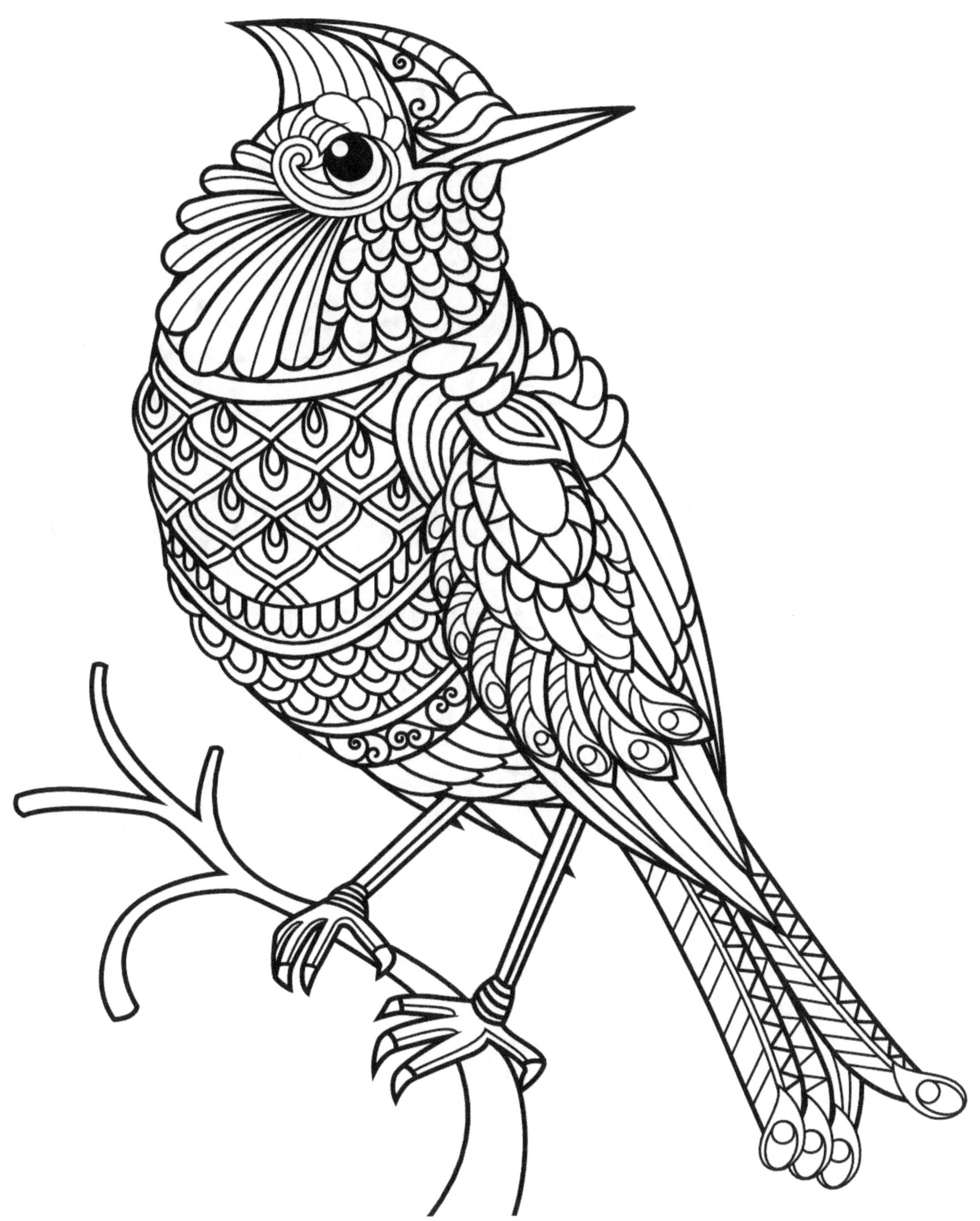

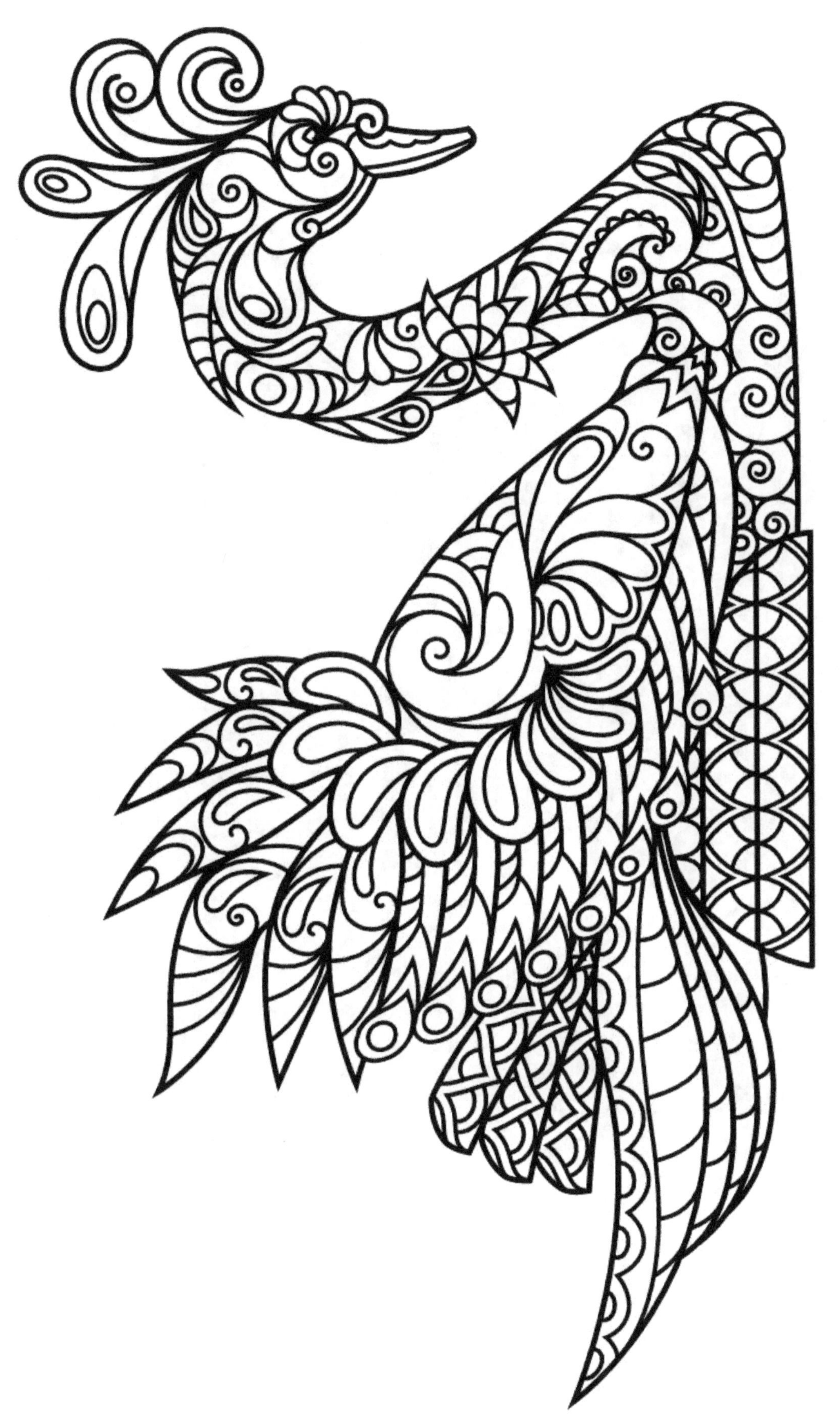

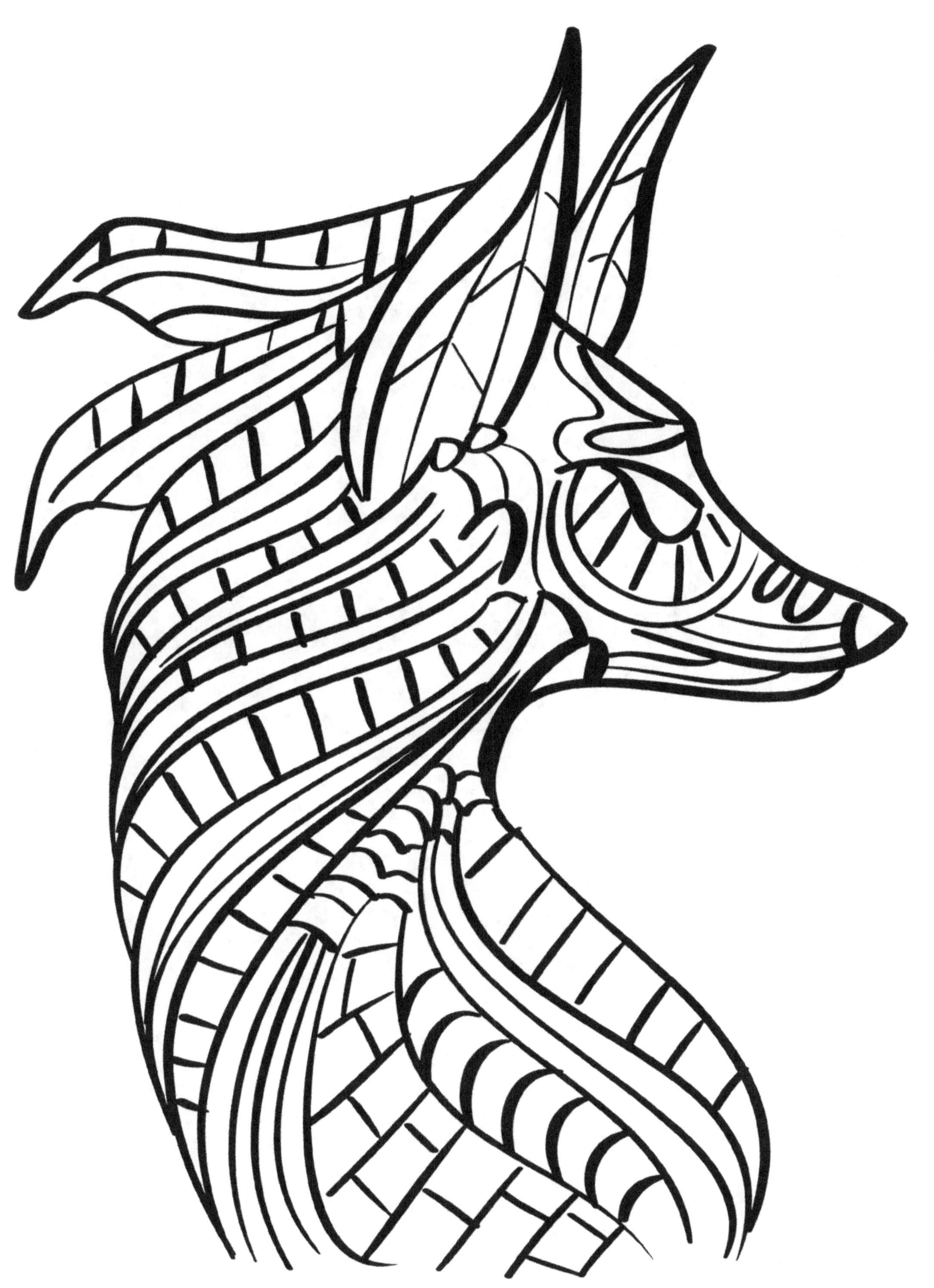

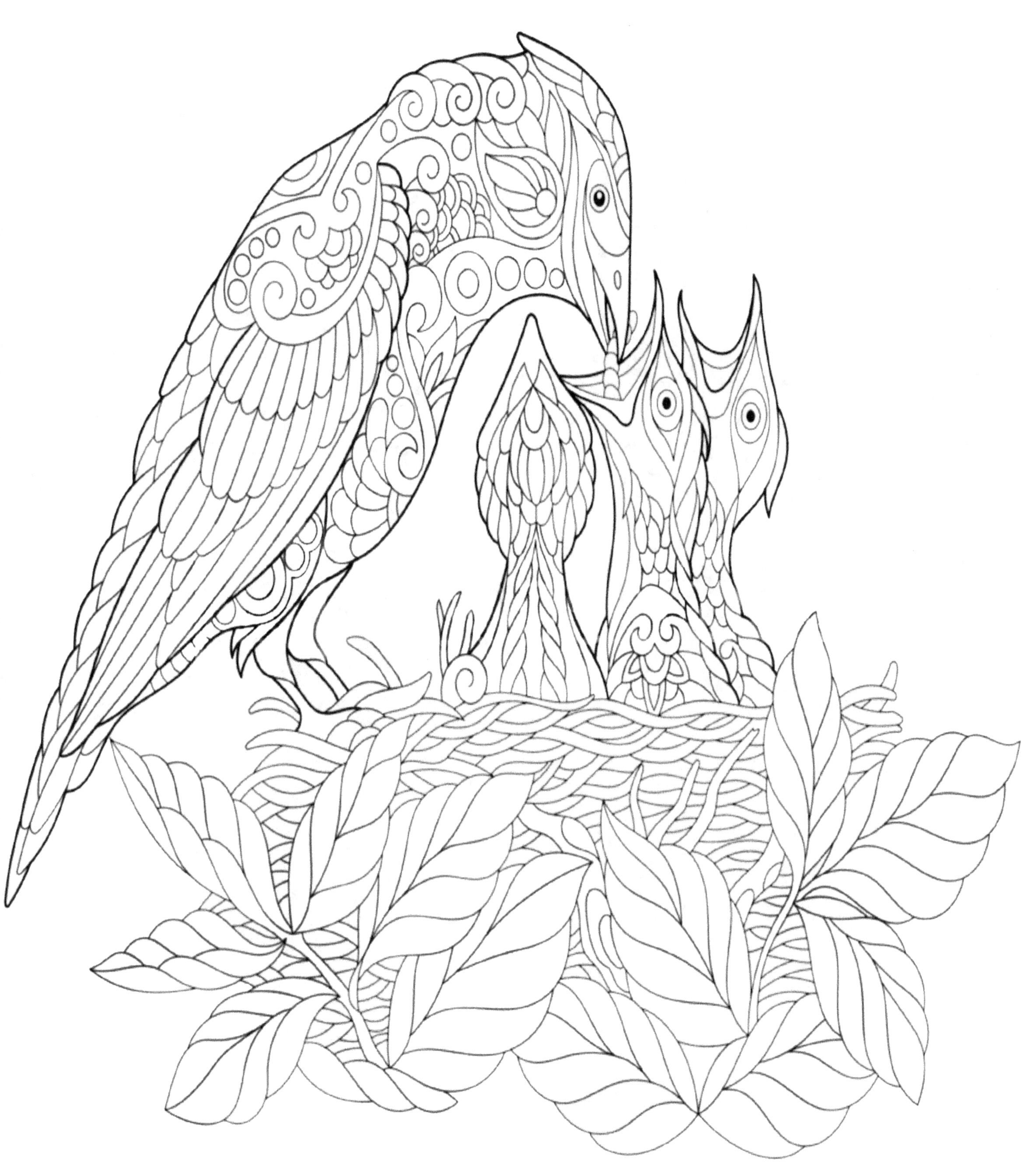

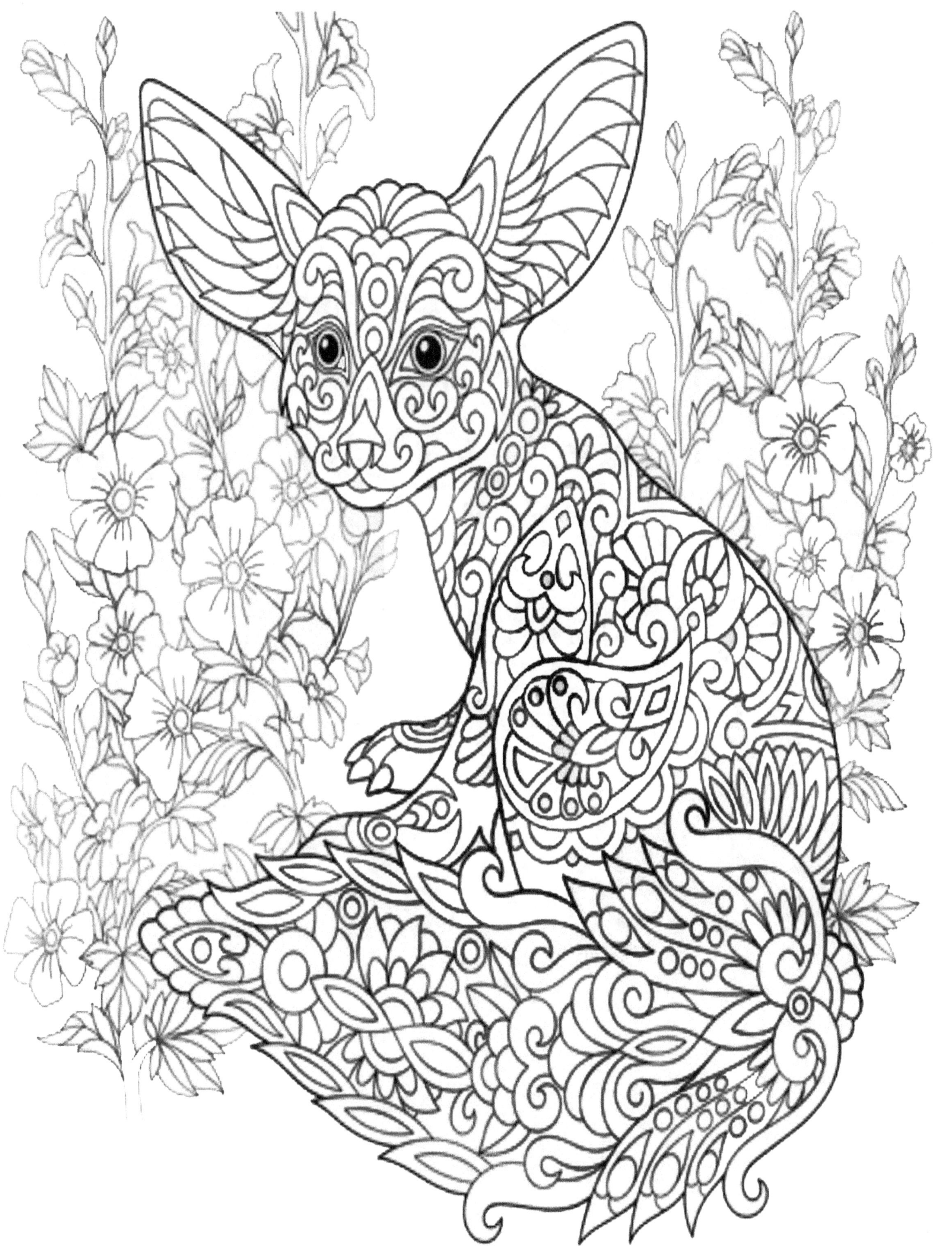

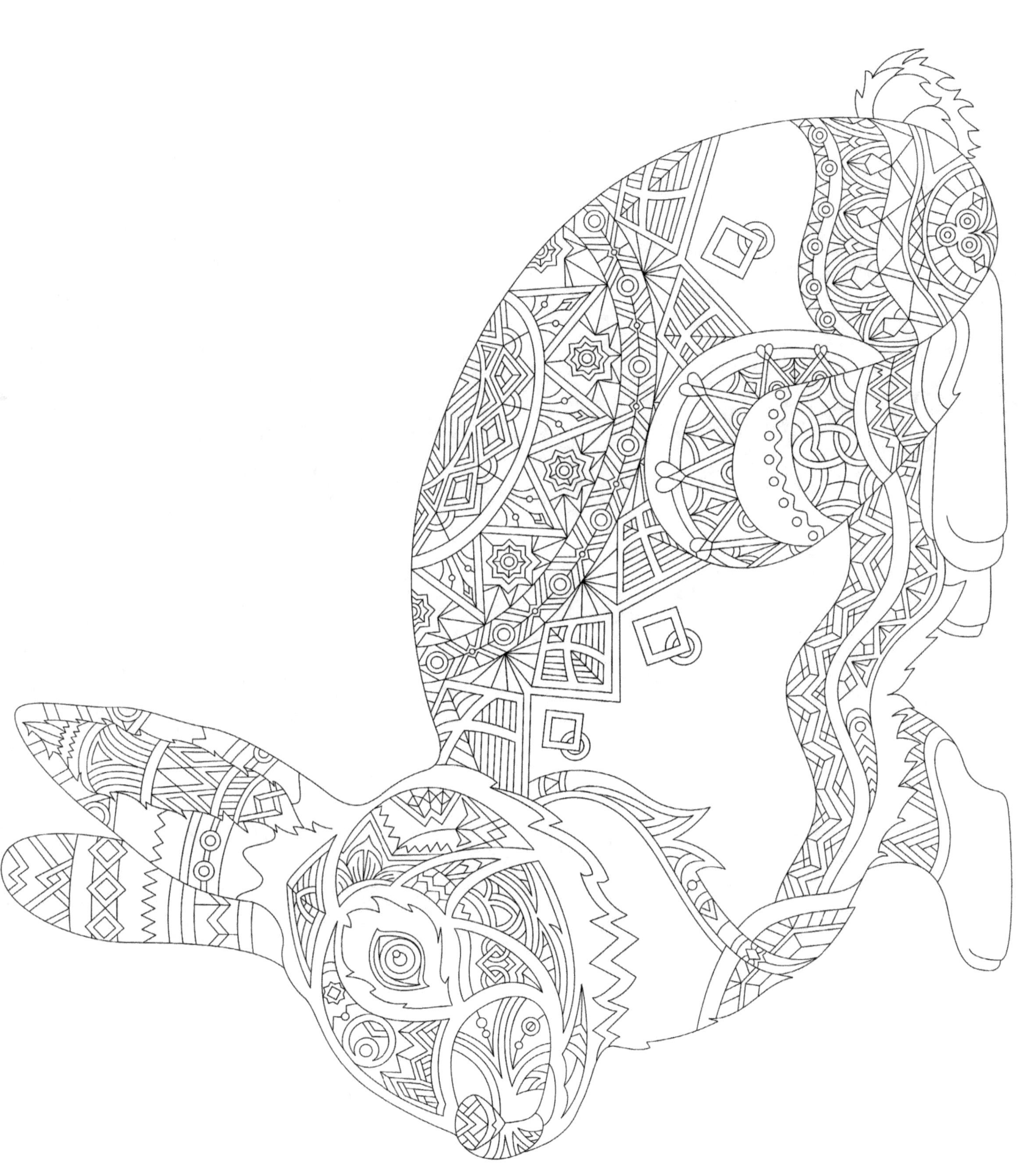

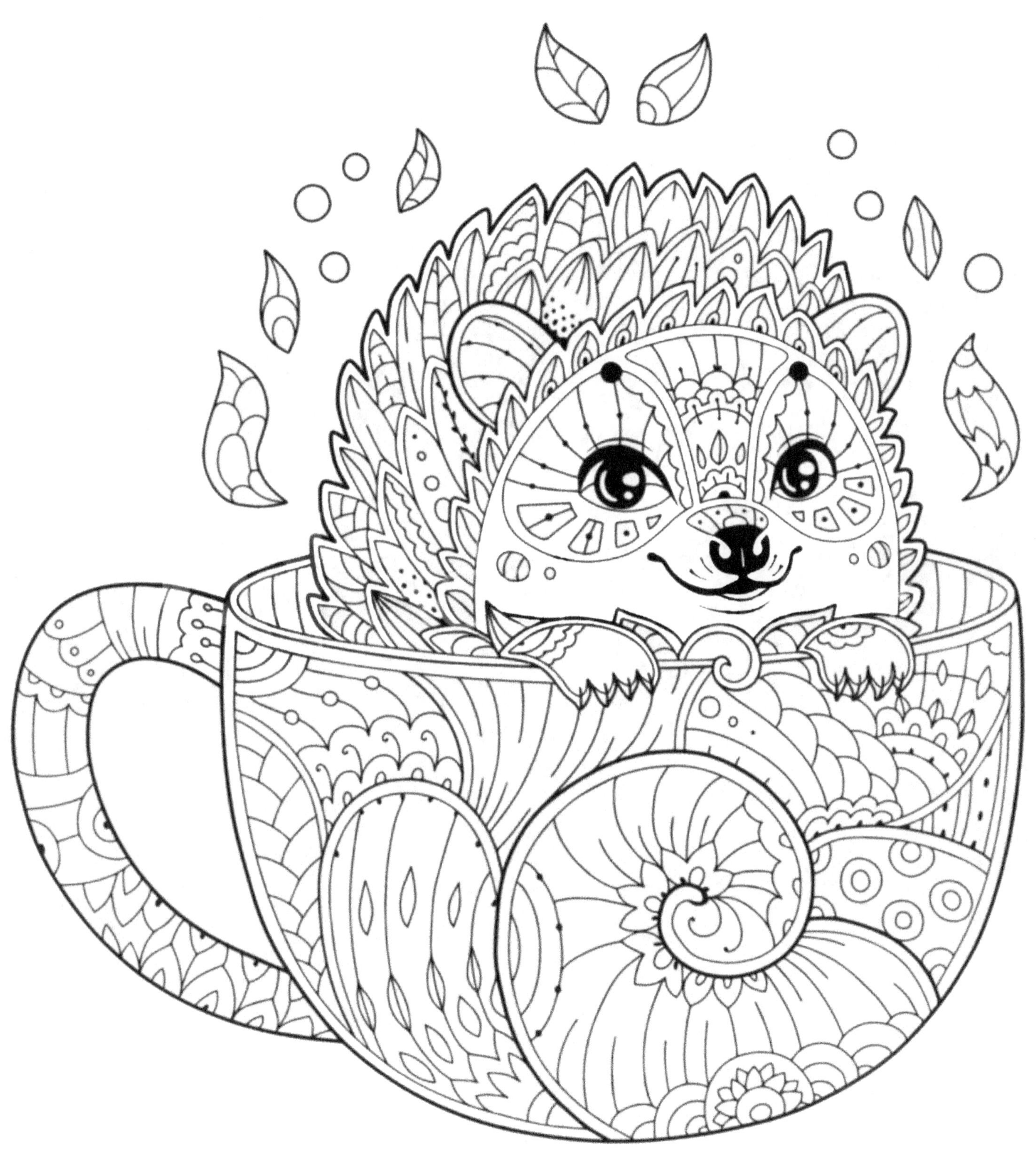

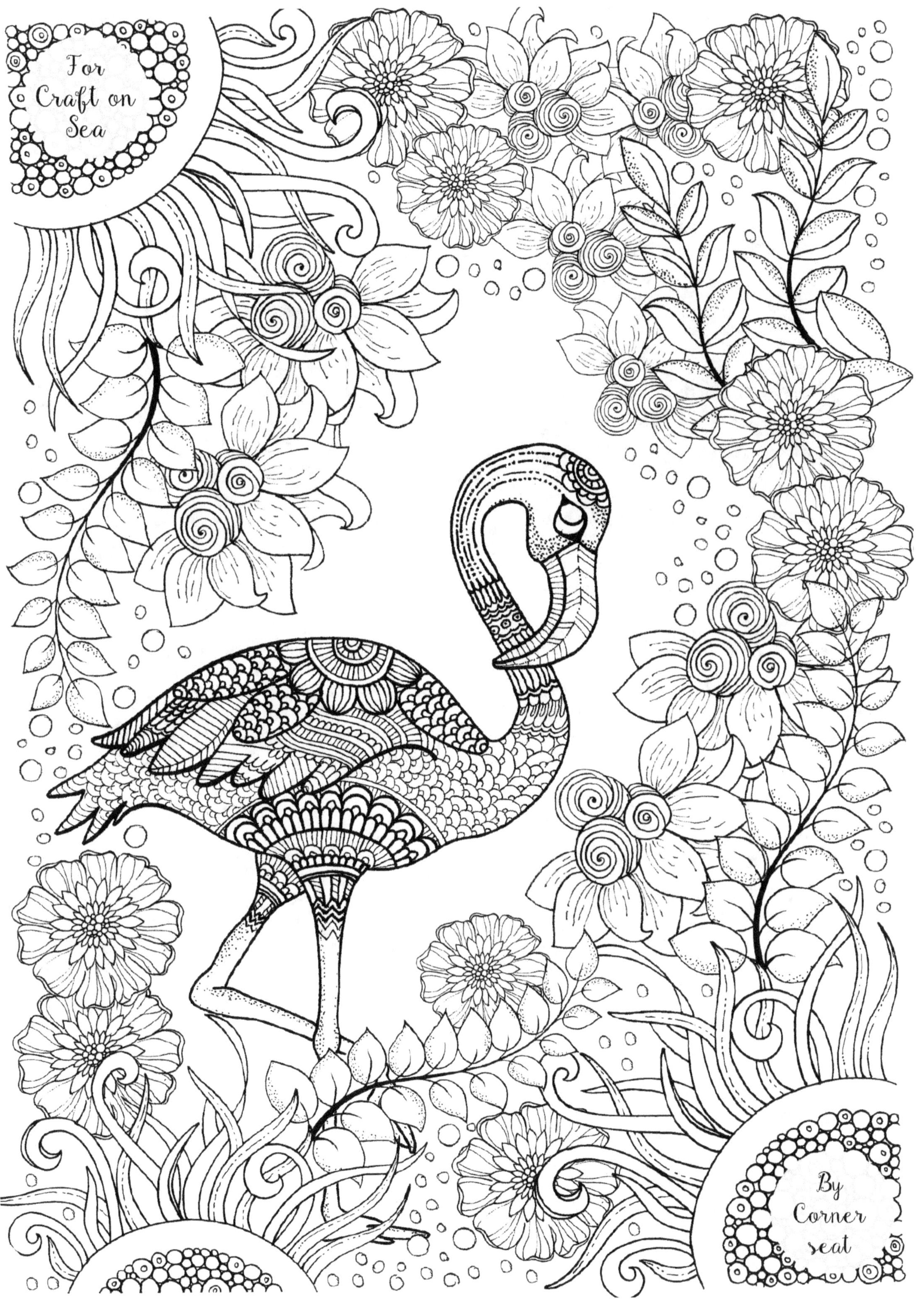
For Craft on Sea
By Corner seat

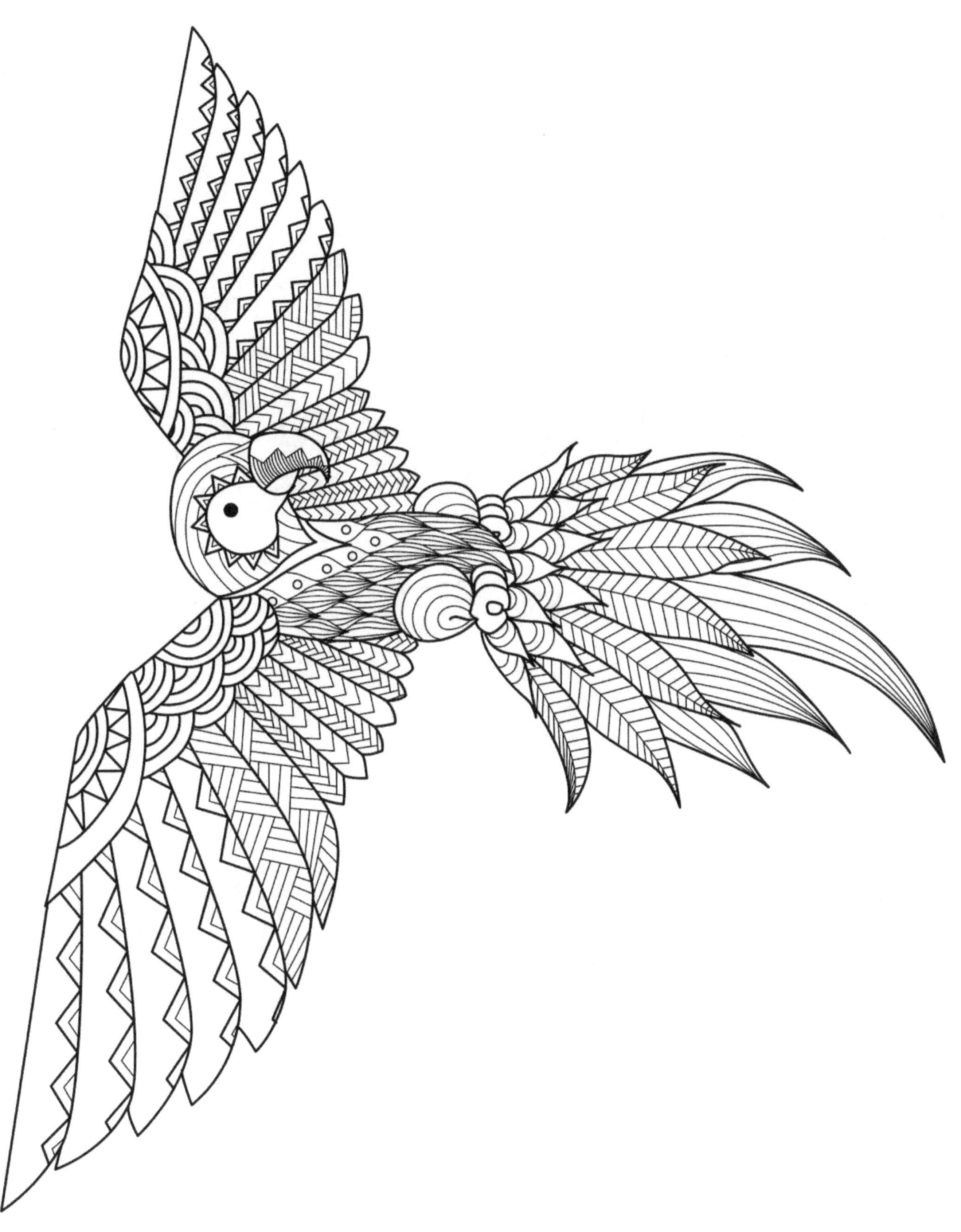

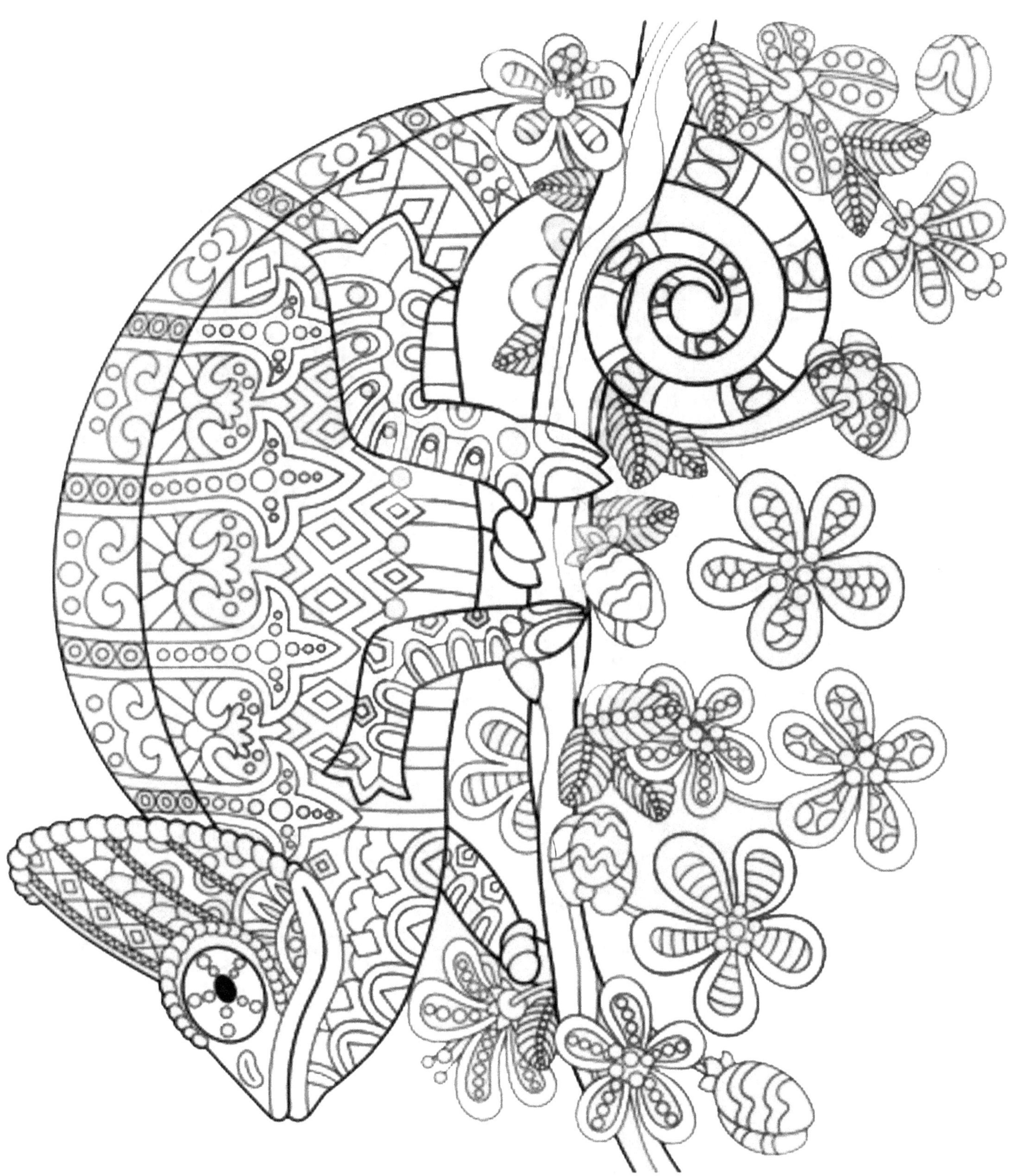

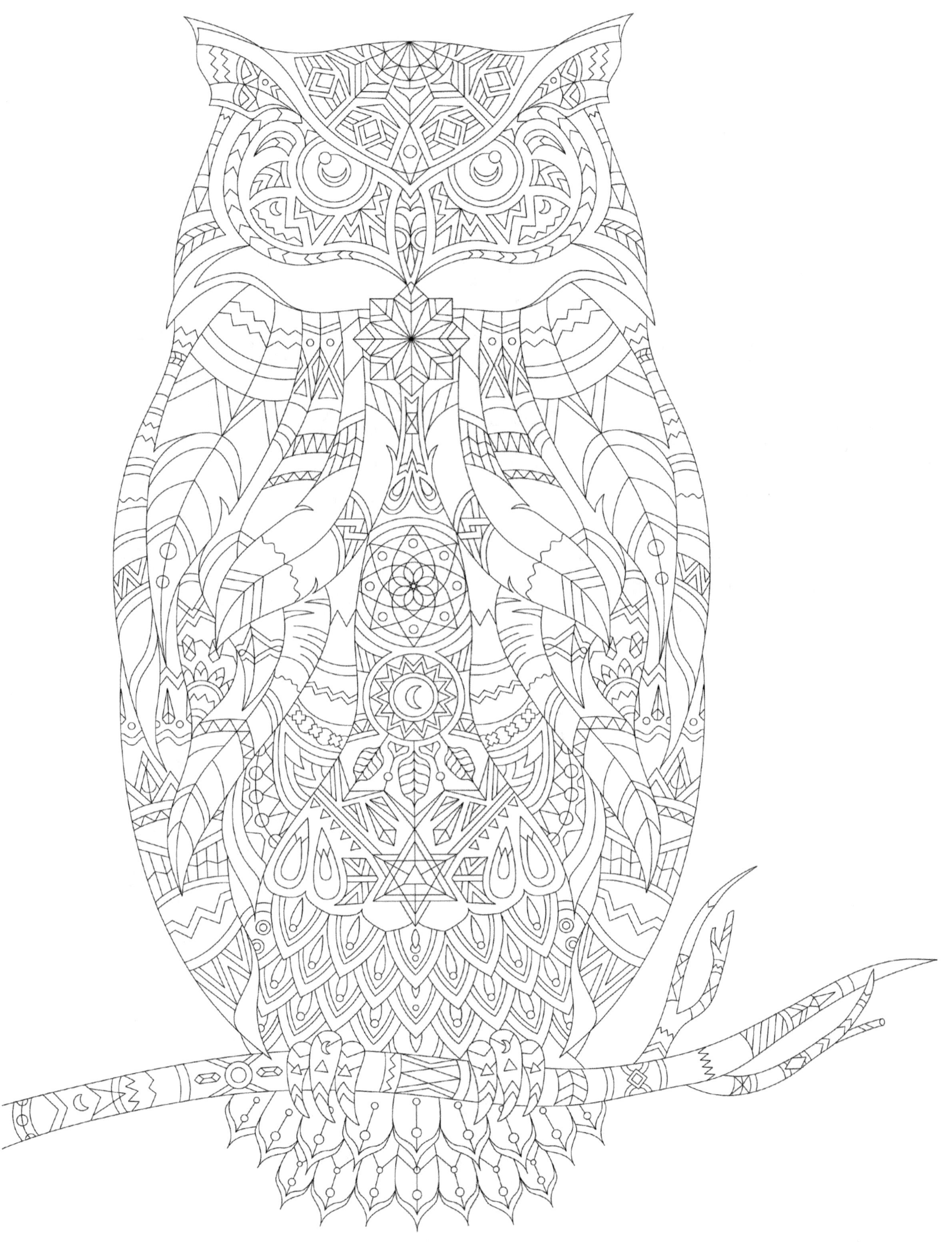

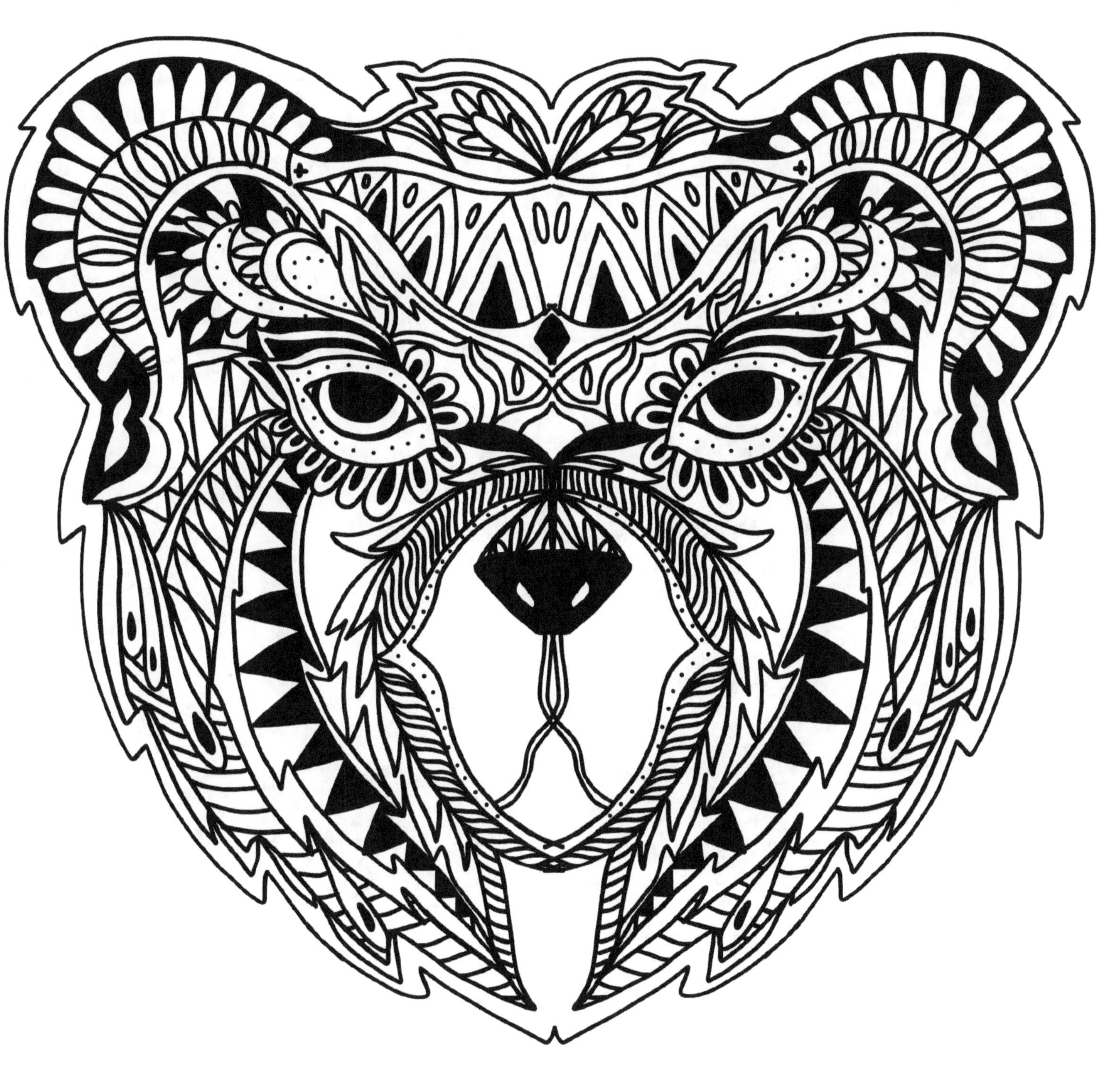

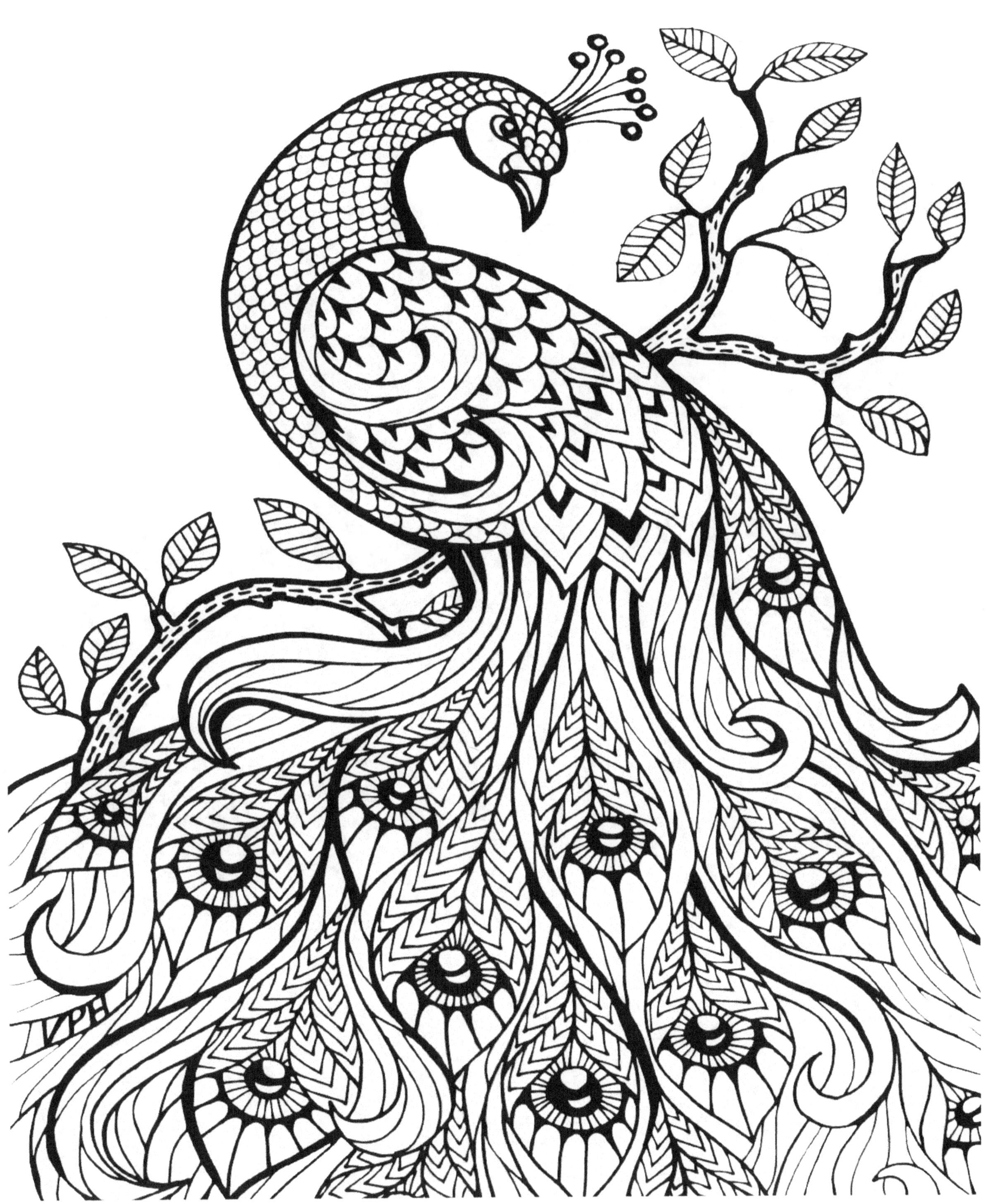

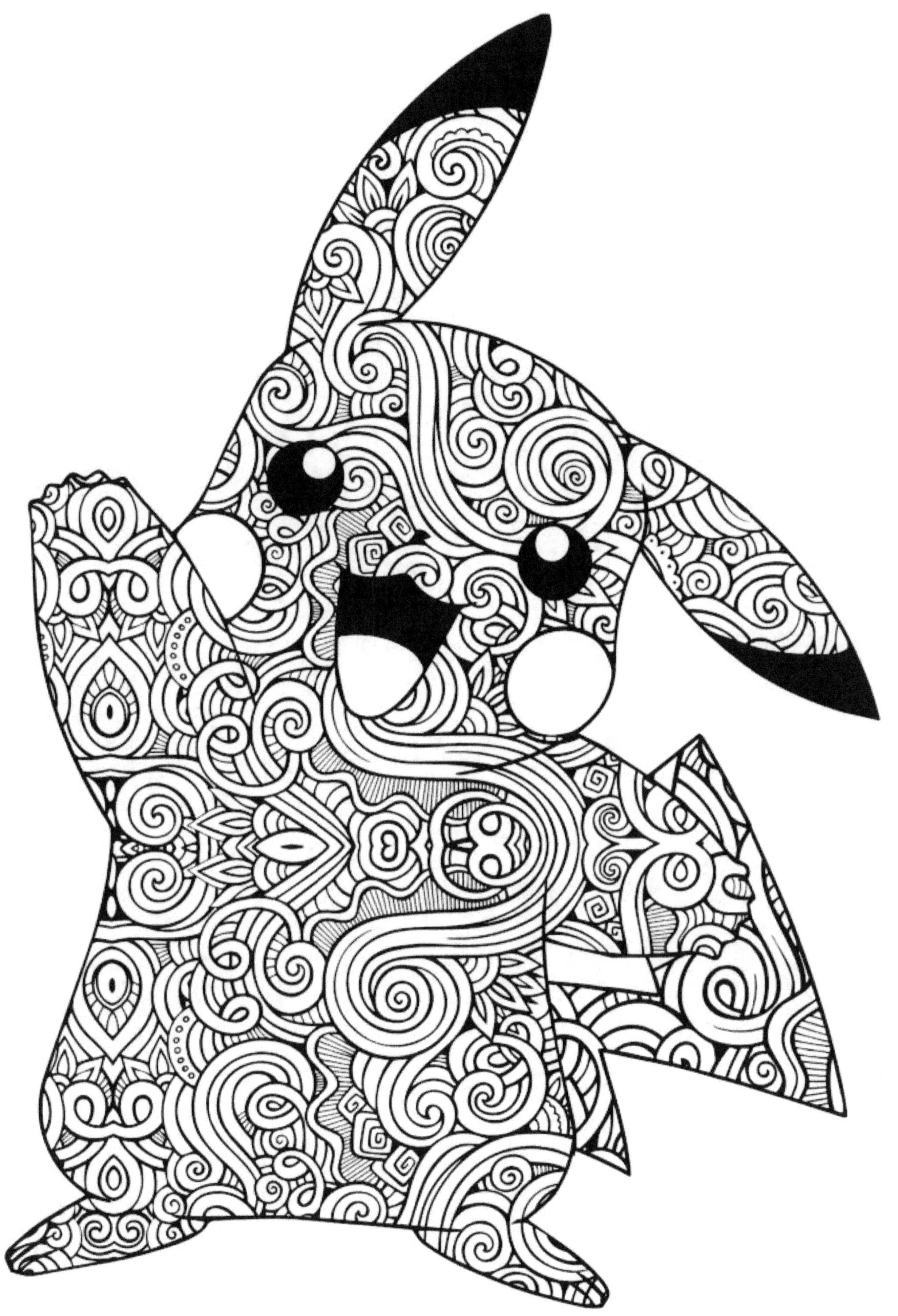